BEN NEVIS

...n Rescue Equipment
in Shelter

Allt Coire an Eoin

Aonach Mor 1219

...rg
...nach

...or
...223

Dearg

Aonach
Beag 1236

Stob Coire
an Laoigh
1115

Sgurr Choinnich
Mor 1095

Sgurr Choinnich Beag

Sgurr a' Bhuic

Water of Nevis

To Loch Treig

...terfall

Binnein Beag 940

JR80

SCOTTISH ROCK AND ICE CLIMBING GUIDES

Lochaber and Badenoch

Selective Guide

A

Rock and Ice Guides
Glencoe and Glen Etive
Lochaber and Badenoch
Skye and the Small Isles
Arran, Arrochar and Southern Highlands
The Cairngorms
The Northern Highlands

Scramblers' Guides
Black Cuillin Ridge
Glencoe Area

Maps
Black Cuillin 1/15,000
Glencoe 1/20,000

ROCK AND ICE CLIMBS

Lochaber and Badenoch

C. Stead and J. R. Marshall

SCOTTISH MOUNTAINEERING CLUB

LOCHABER AND BADENOCH

First published in Britain 1981 by
The Scottish Mountaineering Club, Edinburgh

Copyright © 1981 Scottish Mountaineering Club

ISBN 0 907521 00 2

New Series Rock & Ice Guides: instructions to authors from the Publications Sub-Committee of the Scottish Mountaineering Club, December 1977.

1. There will be a balance of climbs of different difficulty on all crags whenever possible.
2. The selection should be weighted towards popular climbs and good crags and areas.
3. Where a crag exists but has no routes of sufficient quality to warrant inclusion, the crag should be mentioned and a note made to that effect, possibly giving some additional comment.

Printed and made in Scotland by
Hugh K. Clarkson & Sons Ltd.,
Young Street, West Calder, EH55 8EQ

Contents

Illustrations

Diagrams

Acknowledgements

I am deeply indebted to the following people for their assistance in the preparation of this book: K. V. Crocket, I. Fulton, C. D. Grant, E. Jackson, D. M. Jenkins, K. Johnstone, J. R. Marshall, A. Matthews, N. Quinn and S. N. Smith.

The maps were drawn by J. Renny and the geological note was supplied by D. C. Forrest.

The photographers are acknowledged in the photograph captions.

Introduction

This, the second in the new series of S.M.C. selective guides, covers some of the greatest climbing, summer or winter, that Scotland has to offer. To select, from the wealth of routes available, a truly representative selection from each area, has been a major challenge. The popularity of certain crags or types of climbing, e.g. winter routes on Ben Nevis is recognised and catered for, but it is hoped that the inclusion of good, but neglected routes will encourage climbers to sample their delights. Inevitably, good climbs have been omitted. In the absence of the much lamented graded lists formerly traditional in the Scottish guides, this may provide an alternative source of controversy of an evening!

Other changes are in the adoption of metrication and the use of grades above Very Severe for rock climbs and the first tentative grade VI for a winter route. The diehards can shed a tear with the author, but we are in an era of immense change in our climbing world and must move with the times.

If mistakes are found, I would be glad to hear of them for future correction.

As always in guidebook writing, we acknowledge our great debt to the previous authors, on whose foundations we merely build.

C. Stead, Glasgow 1980

Notes on the use of this guide

Classification of routes

For rock climbs, the following grades are used:

Easy
Moderate
Difficult
Very Difficult
Severe
Very Severe
Hard Very Severe
Extremely Severe

Note

These grades are for rubber soles and dry conditions.

The considerable range of difficulty within the Extremely Severe grade compels the adoption of the E grade system, which further subdivides the grade in this guide from E1 to E4, in ascending order of difficulty.

Occasionally, indication is given where a route is easy or hard within its grade.

For winter climbs, the following grades are used:

Grade I   Straightforward snow climbs with no pitches under adequate snow conditions. They may have cornice difficulties or dangerous outruns in the event of a fall.

Grade II   Gullies containing minor pitches, or high-angled snow, with difficult cornices to finish. The easier buttresses which, under winter cover provide more continuous difficulty. Probably equates to a technical standard of Very Difficult.

Grade III   Serious climbs which should only be attempted by parties experienced in winter ascents. Probably equates to a technical standard of Severe.

Grade IV   Routes of the highest difficulty which are relatively short, or longer routes of sustained difficulty.

Grade V   Long routes of sustained difficulty, providing major expeditions which should only be climbed in the most favourable conditions.

Note

Due to the variations in conditions from one day to the next, grading of winter climbs remains an approximation. Much discussion has evolved around this problem, but no more satisfactory scheme has been developed than the current system. Climbs are graded for average conditions, based on observation and experience. Poor build-up is likely to make most climbs harder, e.g. early in the season, while an overall plaster of good névé makes all routes easier. Occasionally, where a climb is considered to be particularly variable in difficulty, a split grade is used, e.g. III/IV.

Routes must be truly under snow and ice conditions to be considered as winter ascents.

The serious nature of winter climbing on Ben Nevis and Creag Meaghaidh must not be underestimated. Bad weather and conditions are more likely to prevail than good. The shortness of a winter day necessitates an early start. Adequate clothing and equipment, combined with physical fitness and a sensible appraisal of prevailing conditions and one's own ability will allow the climber to enjoy the great adventure that is Scottish winter climbing.

A note on avalanches follows (page 3).

Left and right

The terms "left" and "right" assume a climber facing the cliffs, or a gully.

Rope length

A length of rope of 45m is recommended between each climber. Longer ropes can be used with advantage in winter on Ben Nevis and Creag Meaghaidh, due to the paucity of belays. Climbers are urged to use double ropes in winter, as this greatly facilitates a retreat, should this be necessary.

Heights

Heights are given to the nearest metre. The lengths of individual pitches, where given, are related to rope lengths and should be sufficiently accurate. Overall route lengths are summations of pitch lengths. While not absolutely correct, they indicate the scale of the route.

The winter lengths of some summer routes may differ, due to snow and ice conditions.

Rib, Arete, Edge

These terms represent the spine of a half-open book.

Corner, V-Groove, Corner-Groove

These terms correspond to the inside angle of a half-open book.

Litter

Some climbers are notoriously careless with their litter. It requires so little effort to carry one's rubbish back to civilisation, where it can be properly disposed of. The benefit to the environment from this simple act is immeasurable. Please leave no litter, even under boulders.

Bibliography

The Scottish Mountaineering Club Journal, published annually (1890 to date) contains descriptions of most of the routes recorded in Scotland. In addition, the S.M.C. District Guides to the Western Highlands, for Garbh Bheinn and the Central Highlands, for the other areas in this book will be found useful. They contain much of interest about their relevant areas and include some crags and climbs not covered in this book.

Avalanches

An increase in avalanche accidents is occuring in Scotland. Under appropriate conditions, avalanches are common and major ones have even been known to sweep one of the Allt a' Mhuillin tracks on Ben Nevis.

The principal types of avalanche encountered in Scotland are as follows:

1. Dry Powder

Common during and after new snowfall when they can be very dangerous. Also loose, lying snow may be shifted by wind to form the well-known spindrift, which, while unpleasant, is rarely serious except in confined gullies.

2. Dry Slab

Windpacking of fallen snow can occur in a blizzard or where unconsolidated snow is lying on the ground. It tends to occur in sheltered areas, i.e. lee slopes. Snow becomes hardpacked into layers which have no adhesion to underlying layers. A gap may develop between the hardpacked snow and the basal layers. It may then have a hollow sound when walked on and can sometimes be recognised by the breaking away of small slab formations. Digging a section through a snowslope may reveal this structure, but slabs can be metres thick. Dry slab can be very dangerous, as vast areas of snow can break away, when triggered by an unwary climber. Knowledge of prevailing wind and snow conditions prior to visiting a given area may sometimes allow prediction of wind slab formation.

3. Wet Snow

May be loose, or of slab type and occur during a thaw, in warm or wet weather. They can happen to old or new snow. Cornice falls are of this type in spring.

Avoiding avalanches

1. Do not climb during a heavy snowfall, or for 24 hours after.
2. Do not climb gullies during a thaw. Buttresses and ridges will be safer.
3. Do not walk on top of cornices.
4. Where prevailing conditions suggest the possibility of wind slab formation, try to avoid dangerous lee slopes. Seek local advice. Examine the snow structure by digging a section.
5. Avalanche warnings are often given on the radio, in the Scottish news bulletins.

If involved in an avalanche

This is a very frightening experience. At the start, try to jump clear, uphill or to the side. If swept away, try to "swim" and stay upright and on the surface. Keep a firm hold of your axe. The use of a wrist loop, combined with a loss of grip, can turn an axe into a nasty, flailing weapon, which can cause injury. As the snow comes to a halt, maintain, if possible, a breathing space in front of your chest with your arms. Try to break free, especially in wet snow, as it rapidly sets hard and restricts movement. If you are trapped, stay calm and you will use less oxygen. If you escape and others of your party are buried, mark their approximate location and carry out a rapid search. If successful, free the casualty and establish patency of his airways, by clearing his mouth and nostrils of snow and pulling out his tongue. Give mouth-to-mouth resuscitation if he is not breathing. Once breathing is established, give appropriate first aid for any injuries, shock and exposure. If the casualty is unable to walk, secure and mark his position, before seeking assistance. Where the initial search of avalanche debris is unsuccessful, seek help urgently. The chances of a victim surviving burial decrease rapidly with time, although some remarkable instances of survival after prolonged burial are on record.

Geological note

The rocks in the area of this guide were formed over a period from about 1,000 to 350 million years ago. During this time, a great sea, a precursor of the modern Atlantic Ocean, opened up, as the North American and Eurasian continental plates moved apart, then contracted as they moved towards one another again. The sea floor then descended under the edge of North America and mountains were forced up along the edge of the continent, in a manner similar to the Andes of today. These were the Caledonian mountains, a complex chain of at least Alpine, possibly Himalayan proportions. Much later, the modern Atlantic opened up along a slightly different line from the original ocean, leaving this section of the mountain range tacked onto Europe. What we see now are the re-emerged relics of this once great range, eroded enough in places to expose the originally molten roots of the chain.

Ben Nevis

The rocks of Ben Nevis were formed very late in the building of the Caledonian chain. Great areas of lava were poured out onto a floor of schist and, although they have mostly been eroded away, they are preserved on Ben Nevis by subsidence into a magma cauldron. Several stages of piston-like movements of the central cylinder of lavas and schist occurred, with successive rings of granite welling up the sides of the sinking block. The Allt a' Mhuillin path crosses all these rings in its ascent. The 600m thick layer of andesite lavas of the central cylinder starts more or less at the foot of the cliffs. The lavas are fire-textured for the most part, offering reasonable friction. Although the individual sections of cliff vary in the mass, from slabby and fairly featureless, to steep and dramatically sculpted, the climbing is always well detailed, with clean-cut forms, giving direction to individual pitches, if not to complete climbs.

The other centres in this guide comprise Moine metamorphic rocks, which were laid down as silts, muds and sands on the expanding ocean floor, which subsequently toughened with compression and heat. Although these rocks are not normally noted for good rock climbing, they give rise in these areas to some magnificent and diverse cliffs.

Creag Meaghaidh and Creag Dubh

Creag Meaghaidh and Creag Dubh are formed from horizontally bedded schist, which provides, on the latter, the only really worthwhile rock climbing on rock of this age and type in the Highlands. Horizontal bedding creates the rigorously vertical walls, on which, a system of right-angled cracks emphasises the dramatic, square-cut roofs and corners. Two notable features occur on the Central Wall of Creag Dubh in particular. Cleavage in the rock gives such remarkable incut holds that apparently blank walls are climbable and huge, snaking veins of pegmatite cut across the otherwise well-ordered outlines, a hint of what is found to the south-west at Binnein Shuas.

Binnein Shuas

The retiring cliff of Binnein Shuas is on the flank of one of the remarkable series of N.N.E. to S.S.W. fault lines which traverse the Grampian Highlands, this one running from the valley of the River Findhorn on the Moray Firth, to Glen Etive. The greater part of this crag is formed from a massive pegmatite vein complex, possibly associated with one of the many granite intrusions in the roots of the ancient mountain chain. The pegmatite dominates from Ardverikie Wall leftwards, but fades out to the right, until, from Eastern Chimney, the crag is almost solely schist. The climbing on the pegmatite is of a character probably unique in this country, much of it being of a delicate balance nature, on huge single crystals of feldspar. Occasionally, surprise blocks of schist are to be found, such as the overlap at the top of the penultimate pitch of Ardverikie Wall.

Garbh Bheinn

Separated from the other centres by the Great Glen fault (which some authorities believe to be traceable from Shetland to Spitzbergen), Garbh Bheinn is also composed of metamorphic rock. This rock is far from typical of the Moine assemblage, being a splendid, coarse, grey gneiss. Holds are frequently contorted pockets, or small flakes, usually sound, but some of the flakes can be friable. Some highly polished, quartzitic areas of the Leac Mhor can be rather unaccommodating in protection.

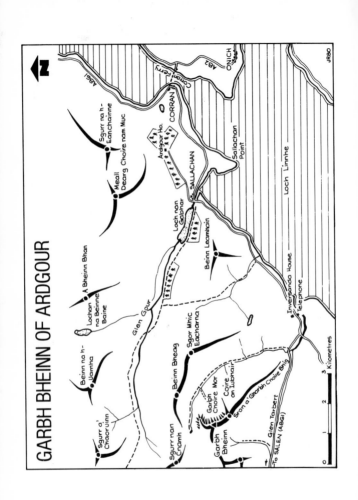

GARBH BHEINN OF ARDGOUR

N

Sgurr na h-Eanchainne

Meall Dearg Choire nam Muc

Ardgour Ho.

CORRAN

Corran Ferry

A861

ONICH

A82

Sallachan Point

SALLACHAN

Loch nan Gabhar

Loch Linnhe

Lochan A Bheinn Bhan na Beinne Baine

Beinn Leamhain

Glen Gour

Beinn na h-Uamha

Sgurr a' Chaoruinn

Beinn Breac

Sgor Mhic Eacharna

Inversanda House

Telephone

Sgurr nan Cnamh

Garbh Choire Mor

Coire an Iubhair

Garbh Bheinn

Sron a Gharbh Choire Bhig

Glen Tarbert

To SALEN (A861)

0   1   2   3

Kilometres

JRBO

GARBH BHEINN OF ARDGOUR

Garbh Bheinn (898m), G.R.904 622, is situated in Ardgour, the rugged district to the west of Loch Linnhe. It lies 2km north of Glen Tarbert and 4½km north-west of Inversanda. The most useful maps to the area are the O.S. Second Series, sheet 40, or the O.S. One Inch map "Ben Nevis and Glencoe".

ACCESS

Access from the main A82 Fort William road is gained by the vehicular Corran Ferry, which runs across the Corran Narrows to Ardgour. This operates during daylight hours and there may be long delays at busy periods. From Fort William, Ardgour may also be gained by following the A830 Mallaig road to its junction with the single-track A861 at the head of Loch Eil and branching off on it.

Climbers are welcome on Garbh Bheinn, except during the stalking season in September and October, when access is not allowed. The "venison cheque" can mean the difference between profit and loss to the tenant farmer for his year and climbers and walkers are asked to respect this ban. Some hind shooting is done in January and February, so if you plan a winter visit then, please check with Inversanda House first.

ACCOMMODATION

There are hotels on both sides of Corran Ferry. Camping is possible in the vicinity of Garbh Bheinn, provided prior permission is sought at Inversanda House (the big house on the north side of the road in Inversanda). Permission is readily given and a small charge is made, the proceeds of which go to the World Wildlife Fund.

Groceries and fuel are available in Ardgour village.

MOUNTAIN RESCUE

For rescue services, contact the Police by dialling 999. There is a public phone box in Inversanda.

APPROACHES

Most of the climbing on Garbh Bheinn lies within the Garbh Choire Mor. This is unnamed on the O.S. maps, but runs south of west from Coire an Iubhair, 1km below the bealach between Garbh Bheinn and Beinn Bheag.

There are three main approaches to the climbs. The most scenic is to follow the good, but wet path up Coire an Iubhair to its junction on the left (west) with the Garbh Choire Mor. A less distinct path leads into this. Allow 1½ to 2 hours to the climbs. To reach the North-East Buttress and the North Face, continue up Coire an Iubhair towards the bealach between Garbh Bheinn and Beinn Bheag, until first the North-East Buttress, then the North Face crags become visible on the left.

A quicker and steeper approach to the upper part of the Garbh Choire Mor, is to climb the unnamed coire, 3km west of Coire an Iubhair, between Meall a' Chuilinn and Sron a' Gharbh Choire Bhig, to the bealach between Garbh Bheinn and Sron a' Garbh Choire Bhig. This is the fastest way to the South Wall climbs (1¼ hours).

The south-east ridge of Sron a' Garbh Choire Bhig may also be used in ascent or descent.

HISTORY

The earliest climbs on Garbh Bheinn date back to the end of the last century, when S.M.C. meets were held in Fort William and it became popular to have a day on Garbh Bheinn. Corran Ferry functioned even in those days and the hardy walked from the ferry, while the better-organised hired bicycles or pony and trap. The first recorded route was appropriately the Great Ridge by J. H. Bell and W. Brown in April 1897, followed only two days later by Winter Buttress by G. Hastings and W. P. Haskett. The latter route was however mere consolation for the first recorded failure in the Great Gully. 1898 saw the ascent of the Pinnacle Ridge by Bell, J. S. Napier and W. W. Naismith, who had been lured there by its sham facade. The Great Ridge rapidly became a classic and had an ascent under snow in January 1908 by W. Ling and H. Raeburn. The lure of the Great Gully remained and successive waves of climbers were turned back, until in 1946, W. H. Murray and D. Scott climbed it in wet conditions. Prior to this, Routes I and II had been climbed on the North-East Buttress.

The mountain was largely left in peace until 1952, when D. D. Stewart and D. N. Mill in two energetic days climbed five routes, including the splendid Scimitar, the first climb on the South Wall of the Great Ridge. It was left to others to realise more of the South Wall's potential, foremost of whom was J. R. Marshall, with the superb Butterknife and The Clasp. The latter route was climbed alone, when the second could not follow. Robin Smith inevitably left his mark with The Peeler and the neglected Blockhead, a typical Smith line.

New routes then became scarce until the intensive explorations of the seventies, when climbs were found on other crags, many of high quality.

The ascents of the often attempted Foil and Pincer were fine achievements, the latter route having been the scene of a notable failure by Dougal Haston as Marshall succeeded on The Clasp.

THE CLIMBING

The rock of Garbh Bheinn is a splendid, rough gneiss which does become greasy when wet. Few winter climbs have been done to date in this area, because of its relative inaccessibility, low height and proximity to the sea.

The best viewpoint from which to identify the various crags, is a short way into the Garbh Choire Mor from its junction with Coire an Iubhair. Where the Choire opens out and becomes defined, past a big, solitary tree, a panoramic view may be had of all but the North-East Buttress and the North Face. At the top of the Choire is the Bealach (col) between Sron a' Garbh Choire Bhig to the left and Garbh Bheinn to the right, hereafter referred to as the Bealach. Below and left (east) of the Bealach are some smooth slabs, the Garbh Choire Slabs. Above and left of these is an elongated, attractive-looking buttress with a number of prominent roofs and grooves, the Garbh Choire Buttress. Lower than this, towards the mouth of the Choire is a narrow buttress in two wings, defined by deep gullies, the Leac Beag Buttress.

Just below the Bealach on the right, or north side of the Choire is a small buttress of reddish rock, Bealach Buttress, bounded on its right by a gully whose right wall is the Bealach Gully Buttress. Right of and above this, and rising to the summit, is the two-tier South Wall of the Great Ridge. The terrace below the South Wall, like that separating its two tiers, runs rightwards to meet the rocks of the Great Ridge which rise to the summit of the mountain. Below the lower terrace, some indeterminate rocks, cut by a shallow, slabby gully at their left end, lead down the Choire, past a small, steep face, then a larger mass of rock at the foot of the Great Ridge proper. The Ridge is bounded by the deep-cut Great Gully on its right. The rather vague, vegetated buttress to the right of Great Gully is Winter Buttress. Broken ground leads right of this to a wide, grassy gully, whose right wall is formed by the very prominent Pinnacle Ridge, which has some steep faces on its left, or south-east side, known as the Upper and Lower Pinnacles. These are merely faces and not true pinnacles.

Well round the corner and out of sight, outwith the Garbh Choire proper, is the huge, four-tier North-East Buttress, beyond which, below the bealach of Coire an Iubhair, is the sprawling North Face.

The crags are described from left to right, as one approaches up the Garbh Choire Mor.

LEAC BEAG BUTTRESS

This buttress is the largest crag, situated low on the south side of the Garbh Choire Mor. It is divided into two wings by a vegetated groove and is bounded on both sides by deep gullies. The buttress name comes from a fancied resemblance to the Leac Mhor of the North-East Buttress, but on a smaller scale. The best climbs lie on the right wing, there being only a 75m route of Very Difficult standard on the left wing.

1 **Dexter**   146m   Severe
L. S. Lovat and C. Ford   July 1954

A pleasant route with good situations. Start at the lowest rocks of the right wing, at a prominent arete.

Climb the arete for 15m and a 9m wall to a stance below an overhang. Climb this directly to a stance near the edge (8m). Follow the edge for some way, until holds lead left to the base of the overhanging belt. Move right below this to a recess near the right edge and follow the obvious groove up left on good holds to a belay (33m). Move right and follow the arete directly to a grassy rake (36m). Scramble to the top (45m). *Diagram page 11.*

A variation start may be made to the left.

2 **Drongo**   119m   Very Severe
K. V. Crocket and I. Fulton   July 1973

This is a fine line, but with some loose and dirty rock. Start 45m up the gully from the start of Dexter at the huge, sloping corner on the left wall of the gully.

Enter the corner and climb its right wall until almost level with a large recess on the left, step right into a groove on the edge and so to a belay (39m). Climb up and left across a steep wall to join the arete of Dexter which leads to a belay (35m). Scramble to finish (45m). *Diagram page 11.*

GARBH CHOIRE BUTTRESS

This splendid, bristling crag lies high on the south flank of the Garbh Choire Mor, some 250m west of and slightly above the Leac Beag Buttress. It is also easily reached by a downward traverse from the Bealach. The routes are described from left to right.

1   The Leac Beag Buttress of Garbh Bheinn

1 *Dexter*
2 *Drongo*

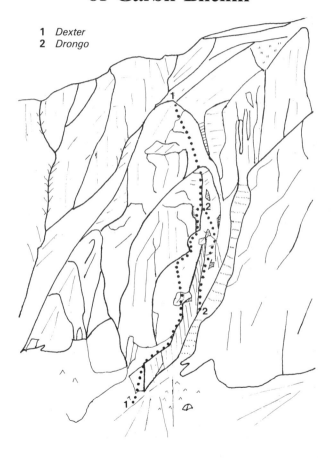

3 **Percussion**   55m   Very Severe
J. Cant and P. Gribbon   April 1974

Near the left end of the crag is a corner crack near a large block.

Climb the corner to a slab, which is climbed rightwards below an overhang, to the foot of a groove with an overhanging crest (flake belay 25m). Climb the groove and overhang to finish. Recommended. *Diagram page 13.*

4 **Swingle**   66m   Severe
A. Matthews and C. Stead   June 1978

Start 8m right of Percussion, at a wall, just left of an edge.

Climb the wall and move right to climb a crack to a grass ledge with a loose block (23m). Follow a broken arete up right to a smooth corner. Climb the left wall, cross an overlap and climb a cracked slab to a comfortable stance at the foot of a groove, capped by a roof (24m). Climb the left wall of the corner, step left into a groove and swing left below the roof, to step back right and finish by the corner above (19m). Recommended. *Diagram page 13.*

A route of Very Severe standard has been climbed between Percussion and Swingle.

5 **Cantata**   75m   Very Severe
K. V. Crocket and I. Fulton   July 1976

An excellent climb. This line lies just right of centre on the crag. Scramble to where a downward-jutting nose abuts on a slab and begin at a loose flake.

Move up and slightly right, then go left and climb a corner to a stance (18m). Climb the corner above (peg runner) to a ledge, then a short wall and slab to a belay at the right edge of a steep wall with twin grooves (27m). Go right under the wall for a few metres, until a good flake leads back left to the foot of a slab. Bear left up the slab to finish over an overhang (30m). *Diagram page 13.*

6 **Cantilena**   100m   Severe
K. V. Crocket and I. Fulton   June 1974

At the right end of the crag is a flying buttress. Start up a corner left of this, move on to and climb a rib to a slab, go up and left, climb an

2 The Garbh Choire Buttress of Garbh Bheinn

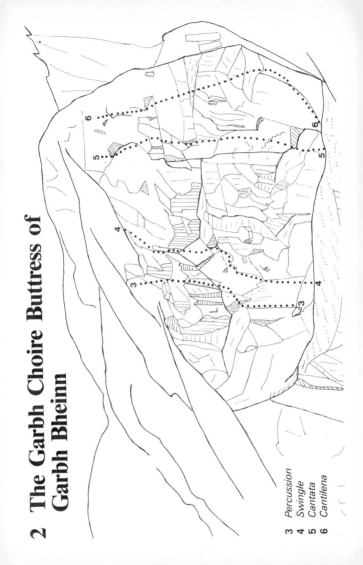

3 Percussion
4 Swingle
5 Cantata
6 Cantilena

1 Percussion, pitch one (Ian Fulton). *Photo: K. V. Crocket*

overlap by a rib and then a second slab and wall to a belay (42m). Climb to a block overhang, pass this on the left, move right and climb a wall on good holds to a ledge (33m). Scramble to finish in 25m. *Diagram page 13.*

GARBH CHOIRE SLABS

These are the prominent slabs, situated on the south side of the Garbh Choire Mor, not far below the Bealach. Several climbs have been made here, but the rocks can be climbed almost anywhere at a standard between Very Difficult and Severe. Climbers can find their own lines on these pleasant, but frequently wet slabs. Not shown on diagram.

BEALACH BUTTRESS

This buttress is situated just below and right of the Bealach at the head of the Garbh Choire Mor. The buttress is made of reddish rock. The rock is climbable almost anywhere and many variations have been made, but only the original route is described.

7 Bealach Buttress   105m   Very Difficult
D. D. Stewart and D. N. Mill   April 1952

Start at the lowest rocks and follow the line of least resistance to the left hand of two narrow aretes which leads to the top. Not shown on diagram.

BEALACH GULLY BUTTRESS

This buttress forms the right wall of the gully to the immediate right of Bealach Buttress. Two routes are recorded here, Sapphire, Extremely Severe, which starts halfway up the gully at a chimney and Garnet, described below.

8 Garnet   57m   Hard Very Severe
K. V. Crocket and C. Stead   August 1971

Start from the gully at some slabs forming the toe of the buttress, below a line of corners.

Climb slabs and a short corner to step right and follow the main corner line to a peg belay (45m). Finish more easily (12m). Two peg runners used on first ascent which are probably no longer required. Not shown on diagram.

THE SOUTH WALL OF THE GREAT RIDGE

The South Wall of the Great Ridge is a two-tier buttress, divided by a terrace. It lies on the south flank of the Great Ridge, just below the summit of the mountain. From the Bealach, a path leading to the summit gives the best approach. The lower tier tapers away to nothing at its left end, due to the slope of the ground, but at its highest point is some 60m high. The upper tier extends further left than the lower and is characterised by two huge roofs. It is about 50m high. By traversing the dividing terrace between the two tiers, the final rocks of the Great Ridge can be gained. The Great Ridge and its South Wall offer the cream of the climbing on Garbh Bheinn, with fine rock, superb views and any sun going. The fact that the climbs on the upper tier finish at the summit adds savour to the climbing. The routes are described from left to right, starting with the lower tier. Some routes ascend both tiers.

THE LOWER TIER

9   Scimitar   105m   Very Severe
D. 'D. Stewart and D. N. Mill   April 1952

This fine route ascends both tiers. Start 30m left of the huge boulder which leans against the lower part of the face, at the point where a shattered ledge curves up to the right. Follow the fault up right to gain the horizontal part of the ledge. From its left end, climb a steep crack to an overhang. Step right to a smooth slab which leads up left to a belay (30m). Climb directly by easier rock and a prominent chimney to the terrace below the upper tier (23m). Continue directly above on the upper tier by a smooth vertical groove and move right to a flake. Climb by a left-sloping corner or the slabs on its left to easier slabs and the crest of the Great Ridge (52m). *Diagram page 17.*

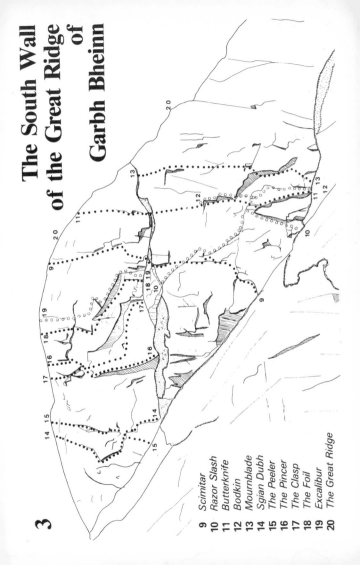

The South Wall of the Great Ridge of Garbh Bheinn

3

9 Scimitar
10 Razor Slash
11 Butterknife
12 Bodkin
13 Mournblade
14 Sgian Dubh
15 The Peeler
16 The Pincer
17 The Clasp
18 The Foil
19 Excalibur
20 The Great Ridge

10 **Razor Slash**   75m   Severe
J. R. Marshall, L. S. Lovat and A. H. Hendry   April 1956

This climbs the lower tier only. Start at the huge boulder which leans against the lowest part of the face. Climb the boulder and a corner to belay on a platform (24m). The platform is beyond the right end of a shattered ledge running horizontally. Traverse left along the ledge for 10m to the foot of a left-sloping layback slab ledge. Climb this, move delicately over the nose at the top and go right, then left to a belay (21m). Go up and left by a diagonal fracture which crosses below the chimney of Scimitar, to reach the terrace below the upper tier (30m). *Diagram page 17.*

11 **Butterknife**   105m   Severe
J. R. Marshall, A. H. Hendry, G. J. Ritchie and I. D. Haig   September 1956

This is a superb, classic climb which is deservedly popular. It ascends both tiers.

Start at the chimney bounding the right side of the big pillar, immediately right of the huge boulder of Razor Slash. Climb the chimney and a corner to belay below a corner crack (24m). Climb the fine corner and continue to the terrace in two pitches, reaching a point below an overhang at the far right end of the upper tier (51m). Climb the overhang and gain the final rocks of the Great Ridge (30m). *Diagram page 17.*

12 **Bodkin**   84m   Hard Very Severe
K. V. Crocket and S. N. Smith   June 1979

This climbs the wall and steep edge immediately right of Butterknife. Start 3m right of Butterknife. Climb to a steepening at 15m. Step left and continue up left to belay on an edge below bulges (24m). Move right and up to overhang, then left to edge. Continue more easily up the edge overlooking the corner of Butterknife (24m). Climb as for Butterknife to the terrace (36m). *Diagram page 17.*

13 **Mournblade**   60m   Very Severe
K. V. Crocket, C. D. Grant and J. A. P. Hutchinson   July 1976

The main feature of this route is a corner, some 12m right of and parallel to the Butterknife corner.

2 Butterknife, pitch two (Ken Crocket). *Photo: C. Stead*

3 Sgian Dubh (Colin Stead and Ed Jackson). *Photo: K. V. Crocket*

Start 6m right of the chimney of Butterknife, at a rough flake. Climb up, then right to the foot of the corner. Follow the corner, step right into a groove and so to a good stance by a pinnacle. Climb a bulge above on good holds and continue more easily to the terrace. *Diagram page 17.*

Right of the corner of Mournblade, there is another, bottomless corner which gives the line of Targe, Very Severe.

THE UPPER TIER

The routes are described from left to right.

14 Sgian Dubh 48m Very Difficult
J. R. Marshall and L. S. Lovat April 1956

This short climb offers sustained interest and fine situations.

Near the left end of the upper tier is a prominent flake chimney. Climb this with difficulty to a platform and belay at its left end (15m). Traverse up left by cracked ledges to a stance. Move left and over an overhang, go back right and climb a nose and steep rock, to finish near the summit cairn (33m). *Diagram page 17.*

15 The Peeler 48m Hard Very Severe
J. Moriarty and R. Smith June 1961

A good climb with some precarious moves.

Begin near the left end of the upper tier, just left of the chimney of Sgian Dubh. Climb the crest of the flake which forms the chimney, to gain a platform and belay (12m). Take a groove on the right and pull up left over a small roof. Go up a short, steep crack which falls back into a groove and continue on this line to the top. (36m). *Diagram page 17.*

16 The Pincer 54m Extremely Severe E1
D. Dinwoodie and R. A. Smith August 1978

To the right of the flake chimney of Sgian Dubh, is a smooth wall and then a prominent groove. The Pincer takes the right wall of this groove, crossing The Clasp at mid-height.

Climb straight up the right-bounding rib of the groove for 21m, then move up left, overlooking the groove and back up right to easier rocks. Go up and traverse left below an overhang to finish up a steep corner. *Diagram page 17.*

17 **The Clasp**   60m   Hard Very Severe
J. R. Marshall   April 1960

The Clasp follows a left-trending line below the left-hand of the two big, diagonal roofs.

Start below the right end of this roof. Climb the wall, moving obliquely left to a belay at 12m. Go on up under the roof for 6m, then traverse left for 9m to a shallow groove. Climb a chimney above, trending left to the top. *Diagram page 17.*

18 **The Foil**   81m   Extremely Severe E1
P. Moores and M. Tigh   May 1978

The Foil takes the steep wall which runs up and left below the righthand of the two big, slanting roofs. The climbing is serious.

Start at a short wall below the right end of the roof. Climb up to the roof, moving left directly below it and follow it until it fades. Exit onto slabs on the left. Belay (42m). Climb cracks above to the top. *Diagram page 17.*

19 **Excalibur**   75m   Very Severe
K. V. Crocket and C. Stead   June 1972

This route gains and traverses the lip of the big righthand roof and offers good climbing and situations.

Start below the right end of the righthand roof, just right of The Foil, at a groove left of a yellow wall. Climb the groove until a traverse leads to the rib on the right. Go up, then left along the lip of the roof to a steep corner. Climb this and step left to a ledge and peg belay (39m). Go left for 3m and climb the walls above to the top (36m). *Diagram page 17.*

THE GREAT RIDGE

This fine soaring ridge, rising to the summit of Garbh Bheinn, is the dominant feature as one approaches by the Garbh Choire Mor. It is bounded on the right by the dark slash of the Great Gully. On the left part of its upper section is a chimney which fades in its upper section. This is South East Chimney. Very Difficult.

20   **The Great Ridge**   300m   Difficult

J. H. Bell and W. Brown   April 1897

The lower part of the Ridge is a mass of slabby rock, which is cut by two grassy rakes. Gain the lower rake by vegetated slabs close to the Great Gully, or more easily, by moving well left, below the lowest rocks and climbing a slabby gully to the left end of the lower rake, which is then traversed right to reach the Ridge proper (this gully leads up left, below the South Wall climbs, so beware of falling rocks when other climbers are there). Climb the well-marked rocks of the Ridge on good holds, with splendid situations and views, to gain the summit of the mountain. *Diagrams pages 17 and 24.*

21   **Great Ridge Direct Start**   105m   Very Difficult

D. D. Stewart and D. N. Mill   April 1952

This gives fine, sustained climbing and, combined with the rest of the Great Ridge is a magnificent expedition. It takes in the lower tier of rock, avoided by the ordinary start.

Start at the lowest rocks, a few metres right of a twisting crack with a slab on its right and well right of a steep, wet crack. Ignore a large cairn, uphill and to the left. Climb a steep slab with difficulty, to gain a prominent, rightward-running slabby ramp with a continuously steep left wall and follow this in two pitches to a broad grass ledge at 63m. Move left round an edge and climb to a second broad grass ledge with a conspicuous flake chimney (12m). Climb the thrutchy chimney and easier rocks to the grass rake. Move rightwards to join the original route. *Diagram page 24.*

WINTER   III

First winter ascent probably W. Ling and H. Raeburn in January 1908. Under appropriate conditions, a good winter climb by the original start.

22   **Great Gully**   270m   Very Difficult

W. H. Murray and D. Scott   June 1946

The Gully lies on the immediate right of the Great Ridge.

Avoid the first 90m by the rocks on the right and enter by a traverse when the gully deepens. After a pitch, the gully widens and is divided by a rib. Climb 10m up the rib and traverse right to a chimney which leads in 21m to a saddle. Move back left to the left fork. Easier climbing leads

C

4 The Great Ridge of Garbh Bheinn

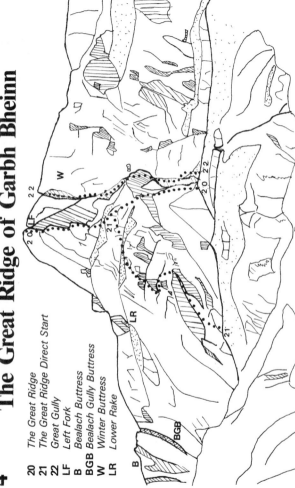

20 The Great Ridge
21 The Great Ridge Direct Start
22 Great Gully
LF Left Fork
B Bealach Buttress
BGB Bealach Gully Buttress
W Winter Buttress
LR Lower Rake

to the Great Cave. Start 18m out from the cave on the right wall. Pull over an overhang by a flake, move right past a bulge and climb parallel to the gully, to finish in 30m by a short wall, just left of the gully bed. A short pitch and scrambling lead to the main fork of the gully. Climb the buttress between the forks, starting to the right. A third of the way up, traverse left for 9m round a nose and continue to the top by the right fork. *Diagram page 24.*

LEFT FORK FINISH   45m   Very Severe
D. H. Haworth and Miss J. Tester   July 1953

The gully forks 45m from the top and the left fork is the direct line. Climb it. *Diagram page 24.*

WINTER   IV
C. J. S. Bonnington, T. W. Patey and D. Whillans   February 1969

The Gully was climbed in its entirety, direct by the Left Fork.

WINTER BUTTRESS

This is the broken, vegetated mass of rock, right of Great Gully. It is of historic interest only. *Diagram page 24.*

PINNACLE RIDGE

This ridge lies north of Great Gully and Winter Buttress. From a distance, it looks impressive, but the apparent pinnacles are only steepenings of the ridge. The ridge itself, climbed by J. H. Bell, J. S. Napier and W. W. Naismith in 1898, offers occasional scrambling. The lower and upper pinnacles have steep faces on their south-east sides, on which are some climbs. The Lower Pinnacle routes are described first, from left to right.

LOWER PINNACLE

23 **Tottie's Route**   48m   Very Severe
B. Dunn and C. Higgins   May 1972

Good climbing and situations, but the rock requires care. It is easy for its grade.

4 Tottie's Route, pitch one (Colin Grant). *Photo: C. Stead*

Start at the prominent chimney on the left side of the buttress. Climb the left wall for 10m, enter the chimney and follow it until it opens into a corner. After a few metres in the corner, gain the left edge which leads to a belay (36m). Climb the corner and left edge to the top. *Diagram page 28.*

24 Blockhead   63m   Extremely Severe E1

R. Smith and V. Burton   March 1957

A difficult and serious climb.

A dark crack runs up the centre of the front face. Start at a 5m pillar, just right of the crack. Climb the pillar, moving left below its top into a shallow groove which leads in some 10m to small flakes. Move left and up to a stance, then up a shallow corner with a cracked right wall. Move up and break out right below a small overhang. Pull left round a loose block to a recess at 20m. Climb by a slab on the right to a belay (36m). Follow an arete on the right to a huge block belay (27m). *Diagram page 28.*

Right of Blockhead, one poor route has been recorded at Very Severe, Bear's Picnic.

UPPER PINNACLE

This scruffy face has three routes, of which only the following can be recommended.

25 Interrupted Slabs   90m   Very Severe

Mr and Mrs G. J. Sutton   April 1956

This climb lies high up in the gully on the left side of the face, not far below the summit ridge. Look for two white-coloured slabs, separated by a big roof.

Start at the corner below the roof. Climb the corner to the roof and traverse right below it (two aid points) to turn the roof on the right. Move up and then left to the edge of the slab and continue across a terrace to belay in a chimney. Take the chimney and slabs to the summit ridge. Not shown on diagram.

5
The Pinnacle Buttress of Garbh Bheinn: The Lower Pinnacle

23 *Tottie's Route*
24 *Blockhead*

NORTH-EAST BUTTRESS

This buttress is best approached by following Coire Iubhair past its junction with the Garbh Choire Mor. The crag is divided into four tiers by three grassy terraces and is some 360m high. The first and fourth tiers give straightforward climbing, although from a distance the latter appears as a formidable tower. The main climbing is on the second and third tiers, the third being known as the Leac Mhor (Great Slab). The rock is slow to dry.

26 **Route I** 330m Difficult

J. K. W. Dunn, A. M. MacAlpine and W. H. Murray October 1936

Start at the lowest rocks at the south (left) end of the buttress (cairn). The route is rather vague. Climb 75m by slabs and walls to the first terrace. Walk up to the main face near its left end and climb 12m on difficult slabs to the left end of a rightward running ledge. Traverse the ledge and climb 80m, bearing right by a series of corners to the second terrace. 60m of slabs at the far right end of the Leac Mhor lead to the third terrace. Climb the buttress above by any line. *Diagram page 32.*

27 **Route II** 330m Very Difficult

B. K. Barber and J. Lomas July 1939

This is a fine climb with a number of variations. Routes I and II share the same approach up the first tier to the foot of the rocks near the left end of the second tier. Climb 12m up difficult slabs to the left end of the ledge of Route I. Continue directly to a stance below the overhanging belt. Traverse right below the belt until the overhang can be passed and the second terrace gained, below the Leac Mhor (75m). This tier is girdled near its top by a long line of overhangs. Start somewhat to the left at a long, narrow chimney and climb this to a stance, just above a huge, semi-detached block at 36m. (The Direct Finish continues above.) For the original route, follow grooves which lead right across the slabs, curving upwards to a stance below a short overhang (43m). The original route now goes to the right up the slabs above to the next terrace. Do not take the corner above the short overhang which is wet, nasty and Severe. The best finish is by the spectacular Turret Variation now described. *Diagram page 32.*

5 Route II, the Leac Mhor (Andy Matthews). *Photo: C. Stead*

TURRET VARIATION   Very Difficult

D. D. Stewart and D. N. Mill   April 1952

From the top of the short overhang, traverse easily left to a grassy niche below the "Turret" or arete. Step left round an exposed nose and climb the turret on splendid holds to the last terrace. Climb the fourth tier by any line, the best being by slabs right of centre. Considerable variation is possible. *Diagram page 32.*

DIRECT FINISH   Severe

L. S. Lovat, D. C. Hutcheson; D. Scott and Miss E. Stark   May 1954

Follow the original route on the Leac Mhor, up the chimney past the semi-detached block to the recess above (42m). Climb the grey slab on the right of the recess, trending left to its crest. Step left into a groove which is climbed for 15m to a narrow rock ledge. Move left and follow the left flank of the overhanging rocks above to the foot of a steep corner (belay). Considerable variation is possible on this pitch below the narrow rock ledge. Climb the steep corner to easy ground and the third terrace. *Diagram page 32.*

28 C'Mola   155m   Very Severe

S. J. Crymble and K. Schwartz   June 1970

An enjoyable, non-taxing climb, but slow to dry. It takes a left-trending line across the second and third tiers, climbing directly the overhanging wall near the top of the Leac Mhor.

Start on the first terrace about 15m right of Routes I and II, just left of a shallow, grassy groove.

Climb the groove and gain the traverse ledge of Route I (27m). Go up a left-trending crack to the second terrace (39m). Move right, up the terrace 12m to the foot of a thin crack which is climbed, crossing Route II at 23m and belay at the ledge beyond (27m). Climb directly to a short, right-trending groove which is climbed. At its top, step left over an overlap and gain a slab. Move a short way up the steep, dirty groove above and cross its left wall and round the edge to a gully, belay up on the right (27m). Climb easy slabs rightwards to the third terrace (35m). *Diagram page 32.*

6 The North-East Buttress of Garbh Bheinn

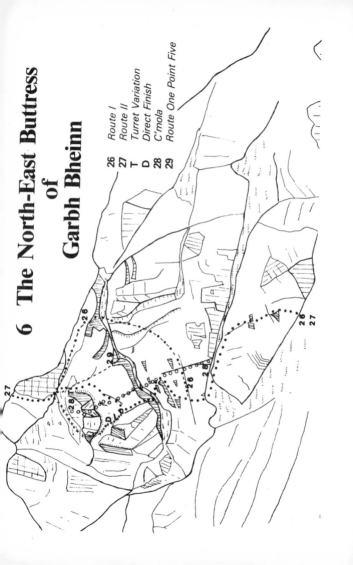

26	Route I
27	Route II
T	Turret Variation
D	Direct Finish
28	C'mola
29	Route One Point Five

29 Route One Point Five 75m Severe

I. G. Rowe and P. F. MacDonald August 1966

This route climbs the Leac Mhor only. It starts from the terrace below the third tier, well right of the chimney of Route II and below the right end of the overhanging belt at the top of the Leac Mhor. There is a recess with a cracked slab above.

Climb to gain the slab and follow the cracks and grooves, crossing the original finish of Route II to reach the upper terrace. *Diagram page 32.*

THE NORTH FACE

The North Face overlooks the bealach between Garbh Bheinn and Beinn Bheag. It comprises some fine masses of steep rock, on which many indefinite routes may be made. The original route only is described.

30 North Face 150m Difficult

B. K. Barber and J. Lomas July 1939

A boundary fence runs from the bealach to the rocks. Start at the toe of the buttress, some 100m left of the fence. Climb directly to the foot of a long, steep slab lying to the right. Cross the slab on good small holds and climb up by its exposed right edge. Continue directly on moderate rock for 90m. Not shown on diagram.

BEN NEVIS

Ben Nevis (1,343m) is situated 6.8km east-south-east of Fort William, G.R. 167 713. Three subsidiary tops are incorporated with the mountain as follows:

1. Carn Dearg (1,020m) is the south-west spur of Ben Nevis and lies 1.6km south-west of the summit.

2. Carn Dearg (1,207m) is the north-west spur of Ben Nevis and lies 1.2km north-west of the summit.

3. Meall An t-Suidhe (707m) is 3.2km north-west by west of the summit.

Together they make an elevated plateau occupied by Ben Nevis and the subsidiary summit of Carn Dearg (1,207m). The other tops bulwark the main mass. The western and southern aspects which overlook Glen Nevis are mainly long, steep grass slopes containing some big gullies and short, but excellent exposures of rock. By contrast, the north-east face falls abruptly from the plateau to present a complex and magnificent precipice some 3km in extent.

Useful maps for the area are the O.S. Second Series sheet 41, or the One Inch Tourist Map "Ben Nevis and Glencoe".

ACCESS AND APPROACHES

There are no limitations to access.

The ordinary route to the summit of Ben Nevis is by the pony track built for the old Observatory. Leave Fort William by the north road (A82), cross the Nevis Bridge and take the road on the right to reach Achintee Farm where the pony track begins. Climb the steep slope of Meall An t-Suidhe to reach the col between that top and Carn Dearg (1,207m). The track from Glen Nevis Youth Hostel crosses the River Nevis by foot bridge, then up the steep slope of Meall An t-Suidhe to join the pony track near the first zigzag on this section. Rising above the Lochan Meall An t-Suidhe at 600m, the path turns back across the distinctive Red Burn to ascend a series of zigzags up the scree slopes and gain the plateau near the top of Number Three Gully.

On the final slopes, the track passes close to the cliff edge where some of the gullies cut far into the plateau. It is essential to keep a watchful eye open, particularly in mist, or in winter when large cornices project far over the precipice.

To reach the Charles Inglis Clark Memorial Hut, leave the track above Lochan Meall An t-Suidhe and continue northward keeping almost level to the far slopes of the bealach. Here, a path will be found which, after descending 30m, bears north-east to contour under the northern face of Carn Dearg. A large boulder, known as the Luncheon Stone will be seen on the left of the track. The Hut is located beyond at a height of 670m, close to the Allt a'Mhuilinn, just above its junction with the burn from the Lochan na Ciste.

Although not a right of way, the old Banavie route can also be used to approach the C.I.C. Hut. Start from the distillery near Lochy Bridge on the A82 and cross the main railway line, where a well-defined track leads to the line of a former small gauge railway. Follow this left for a few hundred metres, cross a small bridge and turn diagonally left up the slope on the right to reach the Allt a'Mhuilinn at a small dam. Cross the burn and follow a track on the left to reach the Hut. Excellent views of the cliffs are obtained from this approach.

An alternative start to this route can be made 1.6km east of the distillery. Cross the golf course and the line of the small gauge railway at a point just left of the Allt a'Mhuilinn. Follow the left side of the burn to the small dam where the distillery track comes in from the other bank.

The walk to the Hut with a weekend pack takes about 2½ hours by the Achintee route and 2 hours by the distillery track.

From Steall in upper Glen Nevis, follow the Allt Coire Giubhsachan for 1½km or so, then bear north-west to cross the Carn Mor Dearg Arete and descend into Coire Leis to reach the foot of the cliffs, or the C.I.C. Hut. To gain the summit of Ben Nevis, bear west from the Arete.

ACCOMMODATION

Accommodation is available in the S.Y.H.A. Hostel in Glen Nevis, Steall Cottage (J.M.C.S.) in upper Glen Nevis, or the C.I.C. Hut (S.M.C.) by the Allt a'Mhuilinn, under the north face of Ben Nevis. Prior booking is necessary for these Huts. Hotel accommodation is available in Fort William and good campsites exist along Glen Nevis. Campsites by the Allt a'Mhuilinn are poor and exposed.

MOUNTAIN RESCUE

Summon help from Fort William Police—telephone Fort William 561, or dial 999.

There are three rescue kits in the area, at C.I.C. Hut G.R. 167 724, where there is also a telephone to the Police in an open cubicle by the door; at Steall Hut, G.R. 178 684; and in Fort William Police Station at the south end of the town.

Small shelters have been erected to give cover to benighted or injured climbers. Two of these are located on the plateau, at Carn Dearg, G.R. 158 719 and Ben Nevis G.R. 167 713. The third is in Coire Leis, G.R. 173 714. These shelters can be badly snowed up, or buried and extremely difficult to locate in adverse conditions.

THE CLIMBING

The location and altitude of Ben Nevis, in association with the Atlantic weather systems, produce great precipitation and frequent changes of temperature and wind to produce snow and ice conditions particularly suited to winter climbing. In itself this hardly warrants attention, but in combination with the superbly articulated character of the mountain's great ridges and gullies, they create a winter climbing environment without equal in the country.

Notwithstanding winter's duration and the mountain's meteorological vulnerability, the cliffs do provide a superb variety of rock climbs of excellent quality and alpine length.

TOPOGRAPHY

Approaching Ben Nevis by the Allt a'Mhuilinn, one passes the huge, broken North Wall of Castle Ridge, then under the Ridge itself which projects low down into the glen to define the wall on its left. Between Castle Ridge and the Great Buttress of Carn Dearg lies the Castle Coire which contains the buttress of The Castle, well demarcated by the North and South Castle Gullies. Raeburn's Buttress lies left of The Castle and above the flake-like Cousins' Buttress which joins the North Wall of Carn Dearg Buttress. To the left, less steep rocks extend to the impressive, vertical or overhanging front of the Great, or Carn Dearg Buttress.

Beyond, scree slopes lead up to Number Five Gully, after which Moonlight and the complex of the Trident Buttresses extend to Number Four Gully, then left under the castellated Creag Coire na Ciste to Number Three Gully, the arbitrary dividing line between Carn Dearg and Ben Nevis proper. Here, the cliffs bend at a wide angle so that the precipice of Ben Nevis faces almost due north. Adjoining Number Three Gully is Number Three Gully Buttress, then the jagged buttress of The Comb, Number Two Gully and numerous minor buttresses which lead round to the Tower Ridge. This is the first major ridge of Ben Nevis and it projects north-east, far into the glen to terminate in the Douglas Boulder. The cirque of crags from the Great Buttress of Carn

Dearg to Tower Ridge encloses Coire na Ciste with its tiny, green lochan set amid splendid mountain scenery.

East of Tower Ridge, the great Observatory Gully (Number One Gully) branches in its upper third to form Tower Gully on the west and Gardyloo Gully on the east, with Gardyloo Buttress between. Further to the east lie Observatory Buttress, then Point Five Gully and Observatory Ridge, followed by Zero Gully which divides the Ridge from the great mass of the North-East Buttress. This projects far into the glen to end in a rocky platform, not unlike the Douglas Boulder in formation. Beyond this is Coire Leis which is bounded to the south-east by the crescent-shaped Carn Mor Dearg Arete.

The summit plateau is a large area with comparatively gentle slopes. A good idea of the configuration of the mountain can be gained by following the edge of the plateau. From the top of Castle Ridge to the top of Carn Dearg N.W. is about 400m. It is a further 800m from its cairn to the top of Number Three Gully, sloping gently down, then up and down. Thereafter, about the same distance and a rise of 150m lead to the top of Ben Nevis. The Observatory is a few metres from the cairn, just behind the top of Observatory Buttress. The Observatory lies about midway between the tops of Tower Ridge and North-East Buttress, which are respectively 250 and 300m distant.

The Arete leading to Carn Mor Dearg leaves Ben Nevis about 300m beyond the top of North-East Buttress. To find the Arete in mist, steer 130 degrees (true) from the Observatory for 365m, descending somewhat, then turn due east. In view of numerous tragedies that have occurred on this route, marker poles have been erected to safeguard parties making the descent. The bearing from the summit must be maintained and on no account should a deviation to the left be allowed. The Arete gradually curves round to the left, until its direction is due north leading to the summit of Carn Mor Dearg. Magnificent views of the Ben Nevis cliffs may be obtained from this peak and from the continuation of its ridge to Carn Beag Dearg. On the south-east side of the Carn Mor Dearg Arete, Coire Giubhsachan leads down to Steall in Upper Glen Nevis.

DESCENTS FROM THE SUMMIT PLATEAU

1. Descend the Carn Mor Dearg Arete (see above), following the line of marker posts to the col between Ben Nevis and Carn Mor Dearg. A line of abseil posts has been erected to facilitate the descent into Coire Leis, but these are situated slightly right of the best descent and are of dubious value except in emergency.

2. Follow the line of the plateau, keeping clear of cornices (Beware of the deeply incut Gardyloo and Tower Gullies) to reach the top of Number Four Gully which is marked by a metal indicator post. Descend this to Coire na Ciste. Number Three Gully may also be used in descent, but its top is less easily identifiable.

3. Descend to the col between Ben Nevis and Carn Dearg N.W. and then to the west to gain the Red Burn area and the pony track. Great care is necessary on this route, as many accidents have occurred to parties who have headed towards Glen Nevis too early. The Allt a'Mhuilinn may be regained by contouring round from the Halfway Lochan. Descent to the Halfway Lochan may also be made from the summit of Carn Dearg N.W.

HISTORY

The establishment of a pony track and summit Observatory in the early 1890s, plus the attraction of the highest summit in the British Isles encouraged considerable tourist activity from the energetic Victorians. However, the most notable man of the period was surely Clement Wragge, who, in the interest of meteorological observations, ascended the mountain every day from the 1st June to 1st November for the two years preceding the Observatory opening.

The earliest recorded ascent by the northern face occurred in 1870 when Number Three Gully was followed to the summit plateau, but probably there were earlier ascents by that route, or Number Four Gully, as the mountain was occasionally frequented by parties from Lochaber engaged in cutting ice for storage purposes.

The first major ascents on the north face were remarkable, Tower Ridge and North-East Buttress in September 1892 by the Hopkinson Brothers, and so discreetly were they accomplished, that the latter route was ascended as a first ascent by several parties three years later.

Encouraged by Collie's splendid ascent of the winter Tower Ridge in 1894 and by the opening of the new West Highland Railway, the S.M.C. held a series of Easter meets at Fort William which accounted for the major ridges in winter, numerous epics and some quite outstanding climbs. After this, exploration continued at a more leisurely pace, with the mountain firmly established as the Scottish winter centre.

Activity consisted principally in the repetition of the recorded lines until the redoubtable Raeburn came on the scene to make his contribution. His excellent eye for line produced among others, the classics of Observatory Ridge (solo), Raeburn's Arete, the ice climb of Green Gully and Raeburn's Buttress in 1908.

The First World War intervened, with exploration at a virtual standstill until Raeburn returned with a flourish to make a hard-won winter ascent of Observatory Ridge in 1920.

Between the Wars, the dominant forces were J. H. B. Bell and G. G. Macphee, their efforts made less exhausting by the erection of the C.I.C. Hut in memory of Charles Inglis Clark, killed in the War. He was the climber son of Dr and Mrs Inglis Clark, mountaineers with a great passion for the Ben and who left a splendid legacy of mountain photographs, no mean feat when one considers the weight of camera and tripod in those far off days!

G. G. Macphee (who made the first descent of Moss Ghyll Grooves, ostensibly to accord with his initials!) was charged with preparing the new guide book and thus developed a considerable knowledge of the mountain, repeating nearly all existing climbs and contributing a substantial number of new ways (all from a base in Liverpool). Although few of these were of real note, he remains significant in the exploration of the cliffs, in that a stirring account of his ascent of Glover's Chimney in 1935, aroused the emergent climbers of the period to the potential splendours of winter mountaineering.

Dr J. H. B. Bell on the other hand, was considerably more selective and, over a prolonged period, pioneered several fine routes including the Orion constellation of climbs, a series of fine mountaineering rock climbs.

World War II, far from reducing activity on the Ben as in the preceding conflict, witnessed the arrival of B. P. Kellett who, from a base in Torlundy was the originator of more than 40 routes or variations over the summers of 1943-44. Many of these were climbed solo in the absence of climbing companions, notably Right Hand Route on Minus Two Buttress and Gardyloo Buttress. Regrettably, he was killed, just as he reached his peak of form and awareness of the Ben, his body and that of his companion Nancy Forsyth being found at the foot of Carn Dearg North Wall. It was a sad blow to the exploration of the cliffs, as he was a decade ahead of his time in boldness of line and, given time, could well have made climbs of a difficulty ahead of any in the country.

Thereafter the pace of exploration returned to normal, with two fine climbs in 1946 and 1947, namely Surgeon's Gully on the south face and the much-neglected Crack on Raeburn's Buttress. Otherwise the Ben remained remote from the dynamic changes taking place further south until the fifties. During this period, the summer and winter lines in Glencoe and the Cairngorms were becoming harder and longer, so interest inevitably moved to the Ben. At first, the great attractions were

D

Zero and Point Five Gullies and many a fruitless weekend was spent watching thundering spindrift wipe out yet another attempt by the "hardmen". Then in 1954, Brown and Whillans, in a rebuff from winter climbed Sassenach, the first of the big, modern routes on Carn Dearg, which focussed attention on the mountain's untapped potential. This event coincided with the newly matured ability of a host of climbers, and a spate of new ascents, summer and winter, was realised, including the then notorious Zero and Point Five Gullies, the former in five hours, the latter in five days, such were the vagaries of winter!

The decade after, the most prolific since Kellett, accounted for many splendid rock climbs on Carn Dearg Buttress and culminated in the development of the now classic winter routes of Orion Direct, Gardyloo Buttress, Vanishing Gully and The Curtain, which brought a new peak of interest to winter climbing and the Ben to a new level of activity. Contrary to contemporary expectations, the great leap forward did not occur and climbers contented themselves with the challenge of new classics to the detriment of further exploration. Then, under the pressure of increased interest in ice climbing, new techniques were evolved using inclined picks and rigid crampons, which enabled the steep ice classics to be climbed faster and less strenuously and gave winter climbing more appeal to a greater following. Numbers climbing on the mountain increased dramatically, as did new winter ascents and the decade of the seventies has seen the awaited move on to the buttresses and walls, where exponents of the new approach have made some of the finest winter lines yet created.

Despite vast potential, summer exploration still lags behind other areas, with only a spurt of individual effort to prevent stalemate, perhaps because of the long walk or poor weather statistics. Fine new climbs have been made on the Trident Buttress, further hard lines added to Carn Dearg Buttresses, notably Caligula and Cowslip and last, but not least, the free ascent of Titan's Wall to provide one of the finest rock climbs on the mountain.

The climbs are described from left to right, from the Carn Mor Dearg Arete to the North Wall of Castle Ridge.

COIRE LEIS

The Coire lies at the head of the Allt a'Mhuilinn, under the crescent-shaped Carn Mor Dearg Arete, the well defined ridge extending from Carn Mor Dearg to Ben Nevis. Access to this from Coire Leis is by the

7   Summary of Ben Nevis

BN   Ben Nevis Summit, 1,343m
CD   Carn Dearg Summit, 1,207m
CA   Carn Mor Dearg Arete
L   Lochan Meall an t-Suidhe
AM   Allt a' Mhuilinn
T   Pony Track from Achintee
O   Observatory Ruin
CIC Charles Inglis Clark Hut (SMC)
S   Refuge Shelters

Route No.
35   North-East Buttress, Ordinary Route
72   Gardyloo Gully
76   Tower Gully
83   Tower Ridge, Original Route
106   Number Two Gully
119   Number Three Gully
124   Number Four Gully
141   Number Five Gully
173   South Castle Gully
176   North Castle Gully
177   Castle Ridge

8

The Brenva Face of Ben Nevis

31 Bob-Run
32 Cresta
33 Frost Bite
34 The Eastern Climb
35 North-East Buttress, Ordinary Route
p First Platform
m Mantrap

south-west slopes, over scree or snow, but considerable icing can occur.

Beyond the line of abseil posts, the rocks steepen into the south-east flank of the North-East Buttress, an area referred to as the "Little Brenva Face" from the open alpine character of the winter routes and, no less important, their occasional exposure to sunlight! It is possible to climb almost anywhere on this wall and indeed in misty conditions to climb for periods lacking detailed knowledge of one's whereabouts. However, the key passages through the final rocks are limited and inevitably lead to one of the established routes.

A small emergency shelter is on the coire floor at G.R. 173 714.

31 Bob-Run 122m II

I. Clough, H. Fisher, B. Small, D. Pipes and F. Jones February 1959

This follows the gully which separates the Brenva Face from a small buttress on the left.

Climb easy-angled ice 30m, then snow to the bifurcation (30m). Either fork can be taken. Each contains a short ice pitch, then snow to finish. The route may be banked up with snow. *Diagram page 42.*

32 Cresta 275m III

T. W. Patey, L. S. Lovat and A. G. Nicol February 1957

The route follows a hanging snow gully which, in its lower reaches ends at a rocky spur some 90m above the screes.

Start well to the right of this spur, climb a raking ice shelf for 76m to gain a small gully which runs up the right side of the rocky spur to its top. Climb the snow gully above for 183m to a large ice pitch, traverse right across steep rocks for 30m, the break through to easy ground above. *Diagram page 42.*

VARIATION 90m II

I. Clough and J. M. Alexander January 1959

The foot of the main snow gully is gained from the left by a traverse across a snow shelf, access to which is by a corner leading to its left end. This is easier than the "raking ice shelf".

33 Frost Bite 275m III

I. Clough, D. Pipes, J. M. Alexander, P. A. Hannon and M. Bucke April 1958

Start from a snow bay right of Cresta and to the left of the steep rocks of the Eastern Climb. Ascend a steep snow and ice groove on the right to reach a large snowfield. Climb this for 122m to beneath a rocky spur. Traverse up right to the crest of a ridge under the steepest part of the spur. Descend on the other side to the bed of a gully, which is then climbed for 30m to the right. Follow the shallow gully to the left, climb an ice pitch for 30m, then iced slabs up to the right for 30m to gain the crest of North-East Buttress 20m beneath the Mantrap. Continue by that route (see below). *Diagram page 42.*

34   The Eastern Climb   300m   Severe
G. G. Macphee and G. C. Williams   June 1935

Start above a large grass slope before the North-East Buttress Ordinary Route traverses the easy ledge to the First Platform.

Climb easy rock for 30m to a 12m wall, turn it on the right and move back left behind a large pinnacle (21m). Continue the traverse above by an easy walk left, then right to the base of a steep buttress (90m). An easy chimney on the left leads to the edge of the buttress, which is followed until the angle forces an escape to the right. Move up, then back left to climb a slab corner by a thin crack under the right wall to gain a large stance on the buttress crest. Climb the very steep rocks left of the crest to a level ledge 0.5m wide. The rocks above overhang slightly; traverse right, round a corner for 6m then up and left to regain the crest at a big ledge with large blocks. (Or climb directly from the ledge.) From the left end of the ledge (exposed), move round a corner into a chimney, climb this, then continue over steep rock on good holds to easier ground. From this point, the North-East Buttress route lies 45m to the right over easy rocks, but the climb continues directly to the steep, final buttress. Climb this by a chimney splitting the crest, or surmount an undercut block on the right wall, then on to the top of North-East Buttress. *Diagram page 42.*

Route Major   300m   III
I. Clough and H. MacInnes   February 1969

This approximates to the line of Eastern Climb and although nowhere technically hard, it is sustained with complicated route finding. On the lower section, the line lies very near the summer route; beyond the junction with Frostbite it goes further left on the Central Spur. Above this junction, follow a leftward slanting gangway (broken by an awkward corner) into a big snow bay. Break out to snow shelves on the right and follow these horizontally left for a short distance to a groove giving access to the upper slopes.

NORTH-EAST BUTTRESS

North-East Buttress, the first of the great ridges of Ben Nevis, extends east-north-east from near the summit cairn, dividing Coire Leis from the huge Observatory Gully.

The lower rocks form a minor buttress topped by the First Platform, a large grassy easement, after which the buttress rises in a great sweep to the plateau.

Left, or east of the crest, the rocks are rather broken and eventually merge with the scree of Coire Leis. The right, or northern flank extends to Zero Gully over the splendid Minus and Orion Faces, an area of great slabs and gullies, encompassing some of the finest climbing in the country.

35 **North-East Buttress** (Ordinary Route)   Difficult

J. E. and B. Hopkinson   September 1892

The route rises 620m vertically to finish on the plateau, close to the summit cairn at 1,414m. As one of the classic ridges on the mountain, the ascent provides fine situations and scenery. It is also possible by following one of the routes on the first step, then the direct variations above to enjoy a climb of more sustained difficulty and interest.

Traverse left below the rocks of the lower section of the buttress until a broad ledge can be followed to the right across the face to the crest of the ridge above the first great step or First Platform. Above this point, follow the narrow ridge to a steepening, turn this by a shallow gully slanting up to the left, then trend right by short chimneys and grooves to gain the Second Platform which is a sloping shelf on the crest of the ridge. The ridge is narrower and well defined above, but presents no real difficulties until progress is barred by a smooth overhanging wall. Turn this on the right by a corner with large steps, or directly, working left from the right corner by a ledge, then a bulge on good handholds. A little higher is the notorious Mantrap, a short step on the ridge, the most difficult pitch on the route. Climbed direct it is Very Difficult, alternatively, an overhanging chimney about 4.5m to the left can be climbed. Its holds are less sound, the exit awkward, and it is at least as hard as the direct ascent. Beyond the Mantrap is the ''40 foot corner'' which is climbed direct or turned on the left, to enter a small gully leading to easier rocks above the corner which lead to the plateau. *Diagram page 41, 42 and 62-63.*

VARIATIONS

The first steep section of the ridge above the First Platform can be climbed directly, or a right traverse made, to climb by slabs and grooves to regain the crest. Both these variants are Very Difficult.

To avoid the Mantrap, the Tough-Brown variant descends to the right and crosses slabs to a gully which leads up to the foot of the 40 foot corner (Difficult).

WINTER   III
W. W. Naismith, W. Brunskill, A. B. W. Kennedy and F. C. Squance   *April 1896*

A winter ascent of the buttress provides one of the finest mountaineering expeditions in the country. Depending on conditions, all degrees of difficulty may be found, with success in the balance until the Mantrap, or adjoining variants are overcome.

Both the original line, or that via Slingsby's Chimney (No. 42) are on steep snow to the First Platform. After this, by following the easier of the summer ascent lines, the ridge provides interesting climbing over snow-filled grooves and short walls without serious difficulty until the Mantrap. This is normally extremely exposed and awkward. Fortunately it is short and, failing the direct ascent, the pitch can be overcome by combined tactics. Alternatively, the Tough-Brown variant on the right can be taken. Above, the 40-foot corner can be climbed or avoided on the left by a small gully which leads to the summit snows.

The following routes ascend the minor buttress leading to the First Platform and are on excellent rock.

36 **Newbigging's Route** (Far Right Variation) 230m Very Difficult
Misses N. Ridyard, A. Smith, N. Forsyth and J. Smith   *July 1938*

Start at the lowest point of the buttress and move up into the foot of the big corner groove bounding the left edge of the buttress (Raeburn's Arete). Climb the slab above and move into the corner to a thread belay (15m). Continue up the slab, pass an overhang on the left by grooves and ribs to belay (25m). Follow the grooves in two 45m pitches to gain more open climbing which leads to the First Platform in 100m. *Diagram page 62-63.*

VARIATION   Severe
G. H. Wiltshire, R. W. Cahn and L. Young   *July 1945*

Climb the overhang of pitch 2 and follow the corner with minor deviations for two pitches (18m and 24m).

WINTER   IV
R. N. Campbell, R. Carrington and J. R. Marshall   February 1972

This route is the natural winter line up the front of the lower buttress. Difficulties should be confined to the first half of the route, but can be serious if thinly iced.

37   Raeburn's Arete   226m   Severe
H. Raeburn and Dr and Mrs Inglis Clark   June 1902

This good route follows the edge formed by the north and east faces of the buttress.

Start at the lowest rocks directly under the arete. Climb to a black overhang, turned on the right to reach a grass ledge and belay (18m). Follow the arete to a belay (33m). Traverse rightwards 6m, then climb up to regain the arete at the earliest opportunity (40m). The climb now takes the arete, with minor deviations to the First Platform (135m). *Diagram page 62-63.*

VARIATION   45m   Severe
A. T. Hargreaves, G. G. Macphee and H. V. Hughes   June 1931

After turning the initial overhang, ascend directly from the ledge by slab grooves to join the original route in 45m , delicate.

38   Green Hollow Route   208m   Very Difficult
M. S. Cumming, E. J. A. Leslie and P. D. Baird   April 1933

From the lowest point of the rocks, work diagonally up rightwards by easy slabs to a grass ledge (18m). Climb a crack on the right, then traverse to a grass platform (9m). Traverse up from the right end of the grass by slabs to gain a groove (25m). This leads to a small overhang. Climb a crack to the left of the overhang, traverse right and belay on its top (18m). Continue by cracks above for two 25m pitches. Go up and right by a slab and groove (20m). Climb the groove to an overhang and exit right to gain the Green Hollow (25m). Continue 25m, leave the bay on the left to reach the arete (18m). Follow the crest to the First Platform. *Diagram page 62-63.*

WINTER   IV

J. R. Marshall and J. Moriarty   February 1965

The slabs and grooves are followed as for summer to reach the snow-filled Green Hollow. From the highest point of the snow, climb an iced slab left on to the final arete, then with little difficulty to the First Platform.

39 Bayonet Route   180m   Very Difficult

G. G. Macphee and A. G. Murray   September 1935

Start from the large grass platform midway between Raeburn's Arete and the foot of Slingsby's Chimney (see below).

Climb a rib of rough rock, trending slightly left to gain a grass niche (21m). Traverse the rib on the left and continue up a grass groove to a belay (21m). Move left on to the rib and climb to below the left edge of the main overhang (21m). Gain the rib on the left and climb until a right traverse leads into a grassy bay (25m). Continue by the rib on the right of the bay in two pitches (36m and 21m). Climb a corner and exit on the left, just above a prominent square-cut overhang (12m). Climb easier rock for 25m to gain the buttress crest. *Diagram page 62-63.*

VARIATION   33m   Severe

J. R. Marshall and J. Stenhouse   August 1959

This provides a direct start by climbing the obvious corner from the left end of the grass platform. Two pitches of 21m and 12m lead to Bayonet Route below the overhang.

VARIATION   36m   Severe

B. P. Kellett   May 1943

From the grass groove of the original route, climb a slab for 9m to a point below a V-notch in the main overhang; gain this by cracks, exit on the right, then, trending left above the overhang, gain the original route in 27m.

N.B. The combination of these variations provides a good direct ascent of the face.

40 Ruddy Rocks   174m   Very Difficult

G. G. Macphee and G. C. Williams   June 1935

Start from the same ledge as Bayonet Route, but a little to its right. Above and on the left is a large overhang defined on its right by twin chimney cracks.

6 Bayonet Route (Ed Jackson).

Photo: C. Stead

Climb directly to gain the cracks (36m). Continue, mainly by the left crack into grooves leading to easier climbing (40m). By the same line, climb to a small black overhang (30m). Turn the overhang on the right using mainly a smooth slab on the right wall (18m). Easier climbing leads to the First Platform in 50m. *Diagram page 62-63.*

WINTER   IV

J. R. Marshall, R. Marshall and R. N. Campbell   March 1967

Approach by steep snow, then climb the grooves which hold snow and ice well, giving a sustained climb for 100m.

41   Raeburn's 18 Minute Route   137m   Moderate

H. Raeburn and Dr and Mrs Inglis Clark   June 1901

This route follows the series of short walls and corners which form the left, or north wall of Slingsby's Chimney.

Start 6m left of the gully bed and climb by the line of least resistance. Considerable variation is possible. The route is one of the easiest approaches to the First Platform of N.E. Buttress from the north-east. *Diagram page 62-63.*

WINTER   II

Climb snow grooves and ledges, by the line of least resistance to the First Platform. The wall, under heavy cover can become a steep snow slope.

42   Slingsby's Chimney   125m   II

C. Donaldson and J. Russell   April 1950

This is the obvious gully leading up the north-east face of the minor buttress to the First Platform of N.E. Buttress. It has no merit in summer, but in winter gives a straightforward ascent on steep snow.

Follow the gully bed until it fans out, then trend left to easier ground. *Diagram page 62-63.*

This can be used as a start to the N.E. Buttress, or, combined with a descent by the approach ledge of the ordinary route from the First Platform, it gives an interesting expedition. The descent of the original route ledge can be very icy.

MINUS THREE BUTTRESS

Minus Three is the most broken of the Minus Buttresses and extends from Slingsby's Chimney on the left to Minus Three Gully, the long, shallow gully raking up left below the undercut flank of Minus Two Buttress on the right.

43 Platforms Rib   130m   IV

H. MacInnes, I. Clough, T. Sullivan and M. White   March 1959

Climb snow and ice just left of Minus Three Gully to a short, iced wall. Climb this on the left edge, then by grooves with minor difficulties to the crest of N.E. Buttress. *Diagram page 62-63.*

44 Minus Three Gully   150m   IV

R. Smith and J. R. Marshall   February 1960

This is the shallow gully raking up left, close under the flank of Minus Two Buttress. The right wall is overhung, but it is possible to escape to the left at several points to more broken ground on Platforms Rib. In condition, it gives a fine climb.

From the gully base, climb mixed snow and ice to a deep cave (30m). Exit by an ice wall on the left to gain a groove leading to the foot of the next pitch (25m). Climb the groove above, finishing by a short difficult wall at 25m and continue on snow to belay (40m). A 15m ice pitch and easier mixed climbing lead to the crest of N.E. Buttress. *Diagram page 62-63.*

MINUS TWO BUTTRESS

Comprising great slabs, the buttress is readily identified by a prominent undercut nose above the lower third. From the lower rocks, a raised crest edged by a great corner on the right leads to the nose, above which, easier rock, climbable by a variety of lines, continues to an apparent tower on the N.E. Buttress.

45 Left Hand Route   275m   Very Severe

B. P. Kellett, R. L. Plackett and C. M. Plackett   June 1944

An excellent climb, easy for the grade.

Climb by the cracks which split the front of the prominent raised crest of the buttress to reach a ledge at the foot of a slab bounded on its right

7 Left Hand Route, pitch three (Bill Duncan). *Photo: C. Stead*

by an overhanging wall (67m). From the left end of the ledge descend the slab for 3m, traverse left round a rib to gain a slab which is climbed on small holds to a belay (9m). This belay can be gained by a direct ascent of the slabs above the ledge. Climb the crack in the corner 5m, then traverse left to the belay, or make a diagonal leftward ascent of the slab to the belay. Both these variants are harder and often wet. Continue up the left edge until it is possible to gain the rib on the right (36m). Easier climbing leads to the crest of the N.E. Buttress at the level of the Second Platform. *Diagram page 62-63.*

VARIATION   60m   Very Severe
I. Clough, D. G. Roberts, G. Grandison and D. Miller   June 1963

This variation ascends the groove immediately right of Minus Three Gully to join the Left Hand Route at the foot of the 3m descent.

Scramble up into the corner which is usually wet, move left, climb a V-groove and exit left to a stance. Go up, then right into the main groove to a thread belay in the corner. Climb the slab, then work right over the overhang to join the original route.

WINTER   V
S. Docherty and N. Muir   January 1972

Follow the summer route, commencing with the Variation Start.

46 Central Route   125m   Hard Very Severe
R. Smith and J. Hawkshaw   May 1960

Start a little to the right of Left Hand Route on the raised crest of the buttress.

Climb by cracks to reach the nose of the raking belt of overhangs above (60m). Traverse right and climb the nose by a thin crack to gain a slab; turn the overhangs above on the left and continue to easier climbing (40m). A choice of routes lead to the crest of the N.E. Buttress. *Diagram page 62-63.*

WINTER   V   A. NISBET & B. SPRUNT 1979
~~A. Rouse, R. Renshaw and N. Williams   March 1976~~

Climb the summer route.

N.B. All winter ascents of the buttress are likely to coincide in some measure on the easier upper section.

47 **Right Hand Route**   275m   Very Severe
B. P. Kellett   June 1944

Harder than the companion Left Hand Route, but equally good. The route follows the line of cracks which lie a little to the right of the well defined corner, which bounds Central Route on its right.

Climb for 10m to a belay in the corner, continue delicately by the slab or cracks above to a small stance (40m). Climb the steepening wall above for a short way, then traverse rightwards for 5m, surmount a bulge and traverse left to a groove which is climbed to a belay (40m). A further 18m lead to easier ground, above which the buttress, although fairly steep is climbable almost anywhere. *Diagram page 62-63.*

WINTER   V
R. Carrington and A. Rouse   March 1972

Climb by iced slabs up the great right-facing corner, to make a difficult exit onto the upper section of the buttress. Continue by slabs and grooves left of Minus Two Gully to the crest of N.E. Buttress.

An alternative, also V, climbs the fine icefall on the right of the big corner to the upper section of the buttress (B. Dunn, C. Higgins and D. McArthur in March 1974).

48 **Subtraction**   275m   Hard Very Severe
J. McLean and W. Smith   August 1959

This fine climb starts 12m right of the Right Hand Route.

Climb the well defined groove for 33m to a peg belay below the left-trending, overhanging continuation of the groove. From the rib on the right, surmount the overhang above and climb to a belay (25m). Climb by the arete to a belay under a corner (40m). Continue by the corner to gain Minus Two Gully at a peg belay (43m). Cross the gully and climb up rightwards on Minus One Buttress to gain the second obvious groove; climb this to reach a belay on a grass ledge on the right wall (30m). Climb the overhanging groove and continue to a belay (43m). Easier climbing leads to the crest of N.E. Buttress. *Diagram page 62-63.*

49 **Minus Two Gully**   275m   Severe
W. Peascod and B. L. Dodson   August 1950

This is the name given to the discontinuous line of deep chimneys defining the buttress on the right.

After 30m of easy climbing, the gully steepens and three chimney pitches of 25, 10 and 8m lead to the foot of a well defined groove, topped by a triangular, black overhang. Climb to the overhang, then using holds above, traverse left to a stance (25m). This pitch is often greasy. Less difficult climbing leads in 60m to a series of greasy chimneys. Climb these, turning the overhang in the second by the left wall and climb to a large block belay on the left (27m). Continue by the crack above to reach the easy bed of the gully in 20m. A short distance above, the gully forks and the right branch is followed for 60m to easier climbing giving access to the crest of N.E. Buttress. *Diagram page 62-63.*

WINTER   **V**
J. R. Marshall, J. Stenhouse and D. Haston   February 1959

A magnificent climb, not often in condition.

Steep snow and a bulging ice pitch, 10m, lead to sustained mixed climbing by the groove and overhang of the summer line, to a chimney stance. Traverse left to enter the main chimney and climb with less difficulty to steep, heavily iced chimneys above. Turn these by iced walls on the left, then more easily to the bifurcation. Climb by easy-angled chimneys on the left to finish.

MINUS ONE BUTTRESS

The buttress is narrow and defined by Minus One and Two Gullies. Steep, columnar rock leads to an easier middle section, after which an impressive crest, seamed by great grooves imparts an impregnable quality to the buttress.

50   **Minus One Direct**   260m   Very Severe
R. O. Downes, M. J. O'Hara and M. Prestige   June 1956

One of the best climbs on the mountain, especially by the variation.

Start at the middle of the lowest rocks of Minus One Buttress. Climb to the corner and exit right to a glacis (25m). Ascend a shallow groove in the wall to a detached block at 6m. Climb it by the crack on its right, then short walls, moving left to a niche (26m). Step right and climb easily to the top of a vast plinth (20m). Traverse right on to a nose above the overhang and climb to a ledge. At the right end of the ledge is an undercut groove; pull into this and climb it until it is possible to climb a ramp up to the right, finishing at a block on a platform (24m). Move up

E

to the crack. Climb an overhang into it and continue up the wide crack to the ''Meadow''. Stance at the great detached flake, well seen from Observatory Ridge (30m). Climb grooves on the left side of the gully to a small stance (26m). Continue up the corner until one can traverse left across a loose wall into a fine niche (18m). Step left on to the crest of the buttress and climb cracks and slabs above to the great terrace (21m). Climb to the top of a 12m flake, then up the crest easily to a curiously poised pedestal (43m). Follow the narrow, shattered arete beyond to join the N.E. Buttress above the Second Platform. *Diagram page 62-63.*

SERENDIPITY VARIATION   45m   Very Severe
K. V. Crocket and I. Fulton   August 1972

This maintains the quality of the lower section, is a distinct improvement to the original line on the upper rocks and should be adopted as the true Minus One Direct.

Climb the original line to below the wide crack, then move left to follow the crest of the buttress to the overhangs. Find a line through these to reach the big flake and finish by the original line.

WINTER   V
N. Muir and A. Paul   April 1977

Climb the summer route to the ''vast plinth'' at 75m. Take the groove on the left to the overhang, then break out right, back to the summer route which one then follows.

51   Minus One Gully   275m   V
K. V. Crocket and C. Stead   February 1974

This is the deeply cut chimney-gully which separates the Minus and Orion Faces. There is a conspicuous overhang at one third height. Under favourable conditions, it gives a magnificent climb.

Straightforward climbing leads to the major difficulties, where an awkward ice wall leads to a cave below the main gully overhang. Turn this on the left (tension traverse on first ascent) and regain the gully above. The next overhang is also turned on the left. Above, a steep ice wall and fine corner lead to a snow bay, whence the left of two snow grooves is climbed to its end. Traverse into the right hand groove and follow it to a final left mantelshelf onto the crest of Minus One Buttress, as an exciting finish to the climb. *Diagram page 62-63.*

8 Minus One Gully, first winter ascent (Colin Stead).
Photo: K. V. Crocket

ORION FACE

This wedge-shaped face fans from Minus One Gully on the left to Zero Gully on the right. The middle of the face contains a depression which holds snow late into the spring. Easily identifiable, this is known as the Basin. It is a place of intersection for most routes on the face. The name Orion was given from a fancied resemblance of the principal routes on the face to the configuration of stars in the constellation Orion, with the Basin corresponding to Orion's belt.

52 **Astronomy**   290m   Very Severe
I. S. Clough and G. Grandison   June 1962

Start from a grass ledge 15m right of the foot of Minus One Gully, to follow a line of cracks and grooves parallel to and right of the gully.

Move diagonally right to a slabby crest and follow grassy grooves to flake belays (36m). Up, then right to a large spike belay below twin grooves (20m). Climb the right hand groove, then trend right to the corner bounding the Great Slab Rib on its left; climb this to a spike belay (36m). Continue up the corner, then traverse left to a chockstone belay above a smooth groove (24m). Climb cracks to belay at the foot of a big slab corner (18m). Continue by a crack in the slab to a stance and chockstone belay (15m). Climb the flake chimney and corner above to a belay (21m). Move up 5m, traverse right and climb a groove to a stance under an overhang, peg belay (21m). Turn the overhang on the right to follow a crack to an overhung corner (11m). Traverse right for 6m, then trend back left and continue more easily to grassy ledges and a chockstone belay (40m). Traverse up left to a grassy corner and continue left to the crest of N.E. Buttress (21m). *Diagram page 62-63.*

WINTER   **V**
A. Fyffe, H. MacInnes and K. Spence   March 1970

The line approximates to that of summer and starts about 30m right of Minus One Gully.

Climb twin cracks (1 peg) to reach snow shelves leading left, follow these, then a deep groove until a return right can be made to a large, left-sloping corner. Climb this and exit right by a wide, shallow flake chimney. Work up, then right into a thin ice groove and trend back left by walls and grooves. Continue this leftward trend under the steep upper rocks until near the top, where a short descent is made into a steep chimney at the top of Minus One Gully. Climb this to the buttress crest.

53 The Long Climb   420m   Severe

J. H. B. Bell and J. D. B. Wilson   June 1940

A fine classic route.

Climb an easy-angled ochre coloured rib on the left of Zero Gully to reach a small platform (60m). From the left of the platform, a rib leads up steeply to the base of the Great Slab Rib, a prominent feature of the route. Round the rib on the left, then move up to gain the foot of the Great Slab Rib (45m). Alternatively climb the rib direct, or by the groove on its right. Both these variants are much harder than the original route. Traverse right on to the crest of the Great Slab Rib and climb by parallel cracks to reach a recess and belays (30m). Move out and up to the right and climb more easily to reach the Basin (45m). Cross the Basin and climb to the foot of the Second Slab Rib (36m). Climb the rib by the slab edge; high up a steepening is turned by the left wall (or climbed direct Very Severe) to regain the crest, belay (30m). The wall above is awkward and should be turned on the left or right to reach a stance (10m). The climb is now on easier rock and many variations are possible. The original route trends up left, aiming for the base of yet another great slab some 60m high. This is not climbed, but the rocks on its right are taken to a niche near the top, whence a short difficult pitch leads to the top of the slab. Easier climbing leads to the crest of N.E. Buttress. *Diagram page 62-63.*

WINTER   V

R. Smith and R. K. Holt   January 1959

Climb snow and ice to the Great Slab Rib which is turned on the left with difficulty, then up right to the Basin. The easiest line above is probably the Epsilon Chimney, the short chimney at the back of the Basin which leads into left raking grooves and so to the crest of N.E. Buttress.

54 Astral Highway   400m   V

C. Higgins and A. Kimber   December 1976

Follow the initial pitches of Orion Direct (see below) to the Basin. Above the Basin, a groove is seen midway between Epsilon Chimney on the left and the Second Slab Rib on the right. From the top of the Basin, climb a shallow left-trending groove over iced slabs to belay beneath the main groove. Ascend the groove over bulges, then by a steep groove on the right. Continue by a slabby groove, trending left, then more directly to a stance below a short ice wall on the left. Climb the wall, then shallow grooves to a belay. Follow a groove, direct at first, then rightwards, finishing by a corner, to exit on the crest of N.E. Buttress above the "40 foot corner". *Diagram page 62-63.*

55 Orion Direct 400m V

J. R. Marshall and R. Smith February 1960

Although not as hard as more modern routes, this remains a magnificent, classic expedition, giving one of the finest winter lines in Scotland.

Start between the Second Slab Rib on the left and a small buttress to the left of Zero Gully on the right.

Climb steep snow to the foot of the wall, then by an iced slab gain the left end of the broad ledge of Slav Route (30m). Continue by the steep ice chimney directly above to a peg belay below a rock roof (40m). Traverse left, then up by ribs and grooves to reach the Basin in two pitches. Mixed snow and ice lead to the foot of the Second Slab Rib which is turned by an ice wall on the right. Above, left trending snow and ice grooves lead to the snow slopes under the final tower. Climb the tower direct by steep iced chimneys to the plateau at its junction with the N.E. Buttress. *Diagram page 62-63.*

56 Slav Route 420m Severe

Edo Derzag, Marko Debelak and E. A. M. Wedderburn September 1934

An interesting route, but messy in its upper reaches.

Higher up Zero Gully, a rock rib rises on the left from the bed of the gully: scramble up the rib until the rock steepens.

Climb to a small stance at 15m, where there is sometimes a peg and move out right and up to a belay (35m). Continue up right to the edge of a steep slab overlooking the gully, then up left to a platform (14m). Follow the scoop to the left of the rib to a shallow cave, 15m, then move right to a platform. From the right end of this platform, climb directly to easier ground (30m). Continue by the rocks close to and left of Zero Gully with occasional difficulties. Near the plateau, the route bears left to finish by chimneys and corners. *Diagram page 62-63.*

WINTER   V

D. F. Lang and N. W. Quinn   March 1974

This gives a fine sustained climb. On the first ascent a 60m rope was used.

Climb a groove immediately left of Zero Gully, then move left round an ice hose to a peg belay (50m). Continue leftward up a steep depression, move right close to a rock wall, then back left and over an ice bulge to a belay (50m). This is level with and to the right of the Basin. Ascend right to belay below a snow arete overlooking Zero Gully (53m). Continue in four pitches (48, 58, 58 and 25m) by steep steps and grooves, close to, but above the gully, to emerge on a snow slope below a wide, square-cut chimney immediately right of a formidable buttress. Traverse over a groove and wall for 30m to ascend a steep groove to a bollard belay (58m). Finish by a groove on the left, then up below a wall to emerge on the crest of N.E. Buttress, well left of Zero Gully.

57   **Zero Gully**   300m   IV/V

H. MacInnes, A. G. Nicol and T. W. Patey   February 1957

The gully lies in the bay formed by the Orion Face and Observatory Ridge. Throughout, it rarely achieves the character of a major gully, being more of a great, open groove.

It is a good climb, not technically hard, but poor belays make it very serious. It is exposed to spindrift.

Climb the central ice groove to a stance on the left, under some overhanging rocks (30m). Continue, avoiding the bed of the gully by a steep ice chimney above (18m). Traverse into the gully by iced rocks (12m), then climb more easily to a stance below the next steep section (30m). Climb a short, steep wall and move right to a groove which is followed to a stance and belay (30m). Continue by the pitch above (40m), then easily by snow and occasional short pitches to the plateau.

After pitch one, the gully bed may be climbed directly to make a harder climb. *Diagram page 62-63.*

OBSERVATORY RIDGE

Observatory Ridge is the name originally given to the slender buttress right of Zero Gully, but for ease of reference has been enlarged to embrace the rocks extending right to Point Five Gully.

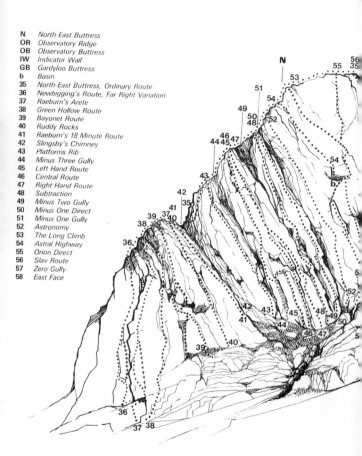

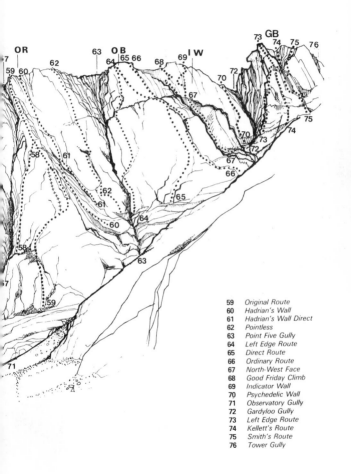

59	*Original Route*
60	*Hadrian's Wall*
61	*Hadrian's Wall Direct*
62	*Pointless*
63	*Point Five Gully*
64	*Left Edge Route*
65	*Direct Route*
66	*Ordinary Route*
67	*North-West Face*
68	*Good Friday Climb*
69	*Indicator Wall*
70	*Psychedelic Wall*
71	*Observatory Gully*
72	*Gardyloo Gully*
73	*Left Edge Route*
74	*Kellett's Route*
75	*Smith's Route*
76	*Tower Gully*

9 Observatory Ridge (Ken Crocket). *Photo: C. Stead*

58   East Face   170m   IV

B. Dunn and C. Higgins   March 1974

Below and to the right of Zero Gully, a prominent groove strikes leftwards for the entire length of the east face of Observatory Ridge. With the groove completely iced up, several bulges will normally be encountered before gaining the crest of Observatory Ridge. *Diagram page 62-63.*

59   Original Route   420m   Difficult

H. Raeburn   June 1901

Summer or winter, this is a really splendid climb.

From the lowest rocks, climb easily to the rightmost end of an obvious terrace at 60m. Continue by slabs and walls a little left of the crest, to steeper rocks, which are turned on the right flank of the buttress (or climbed direct, Very Difficult), then by cracks and grooves to the easier angled crest of the ridge. Follow this with occasional difficulties to the plateau. *Diagram page 62-63.*

WINTER   III

H. Raeburn, F. S. Goggs and W. A. Mounsey   April 1920

The summer route is followed throughout. Generally the greatest difficulties are to be met on the rocks just below the easement of the buttress, but the ascent is quite sustained over the lower half of the route.

60   Hadrian's Wall   325m   IV

W. D. Brooker, J. R. Marshall and T. W. Patey   February 1959

Hadrian's Wall is the name given to the winter ascent of the West Face; Lower Route, originally climbed by Kellett. It is an enjoyable route, somewhat neglected in favour of its fiercer variation.

Start about 30m left of Point Five Gully.

Climb to the base of twin ice grooves (25m). Enter the left groove and climb to a steep snow bay under the vertical upper wall (40m). Traverse snow and iced slabs up right under the wall to enter a deep, ice chimney which leads to the easier upper section of the buttress. Follow the shallow scoop above, then negotiate awkward slab walls under the plateau edge to finish.

On pitch two, the right hand groove may be climbed. *Diagram page 62-63.*

61 **Hadrian's Wall Direct**   300m   V

M. G. Geddes and G. Little   Easter 1971

A popular climb, often in condition.

There is normally an ice smear, well seen from the C.I.C. Hut, which extends from the high chimney of Hadrian's Wall to the left foot of Point Five Gully. This is the line of the route.

Climb the smear, bulges and all in two pitches for 90m, to an easier groove leading up to the chimney of Hadrian's Wall. Continue as for that route, or by the line of one's choice on the upper cliff. *Diagram page 62-63.*

62 **Pointless**   332m   Very Severe

R. Marshall and J. R. Marshall   September 1966

This route follows a central line up the great slabs to the left of Point Five Gully.

Start left of the foot of the gully. Climb a groove leading to a large scree patch (30m). Continue by the crest of a broad rib, aiming for the foot of the obvious corner above, to belay under slabs barring access to the corner (18m). Climb the slabs slightly right of centre to a spike belay under the corner (18m). Climb the corner, break out right and belay under another corner on the right (28m). Follow the steepening corner to belays (30m). Continue by the same line towards a narrow chimney and belay (30m). Climb the chimney to the ledge of the Girdle Traverse (18m), cairn. Continue directly by slabs and grooves for 35m, then, occasionally climbing to the plateau in 125m. *Diagram page 62-63.*

WINTER   V

N. Banks and G. Smith   February 1978

The ascent follows the line of the summer route, starting immediately left of Point Five Gully. It requires a good plating of ice, when it provides a good, but very poorly protected climb.

63 **Point Five Gully**   325m   V

J. M. Alexander, I. S. Clough, D. Pipes and R. Shaw   January 1959

This classic gully offers sustained climbing over its lower half, with good belays. It is subject to spindrift avalanches which descend with devastating effect whenever wind conditions are shifting powder snow from the higher crags. Sadly, one may have to queue for this route nowadays.

Under normal conditions, details are as follows. Climb an iced slab to stance under a wall (30m). Move out left on vertical ice, then right by an ice bulge to reach a snow bay and stance (10m). Climb ice-choked chimneys to a snow stance (45m). Climb by a continuously steepening ice wall, 15m, to reach the easier upper section of the gully. Continue by short ice pitches to the plateau. *Diagram page 62-63.*

OBSERVATORY BUTTRESS

About half-way up Observatory Gully, the buttress rises steeply from the screes on the left. It forms the broad mass of rock extending from Point Five Gully on the left to Gardyloo Gully on the right.

At mid-height, the buttress is traversed by a great ledge, broadening to the right and giving access to the junction between the foot of Gardyloo Gully and the exit from Observatory Gully.

64 **Left Edge Route** 325m Severe
C. M. Allan, J. H. B. Bell and E. A. M. Wedderburn   September 1936

This is a route of character, with fine situations.

Start at the foot of the rib bounding Point Five Gully on its right. Climb the rib to a belay (30m). Continue by the steeper rocks above for 12m, then move right to belay. Climb the shallow groove on the left, then out right and up to gain the "luncheon spot". Gain the flake on the right and move up into a groove and slab (18m). Follow the grassy slab-rake up to the right for 20m. Climb the steep waterworn groove above, moving right to finish at a ledge and block (25m). Surmount the corner above and another corner leading left to the easy terrace. Follow the crest above by scrambling, then cracks and chimneys to the plateau. *Diagram page 62-63.*

WINTER   V
D. F. Lang and N. W. Quinn   March 1974

Climbed generally as for summer, it provides sustained climbing and very long run-outs.

65   **Direct Route**   340m   Very Difficult
A. T. Hargreaves, G. G. MacPhee and H. V. Hughes   June 1931

This is an enjoyable route.

Start 27m right of the lowest rocks in a shallow bay.

Climb 45m to reach stepped, awkward, short walls, which are climbed to a large platform and belay. A series of walls and corners, leading up and slightly rightwards, give access to a ledge with a large slab leaning against the left wall, thread belay. Continue above (as for Ordinary Route) by steep slabs trending right to an overhang close to the chimney. Turn the overhang on the left and climb to a recess and belay. Easier climbing leads to the middle terrace. Move up to the left where 60m of scrambling lead to an obvious crack, topped by an overhang. Climb the crack, turn the overhang on the right and climb to easier slabs. Gain the crest on the left by a chimney and climb to the plateau. *Diagram page 62-63.*

VARIATION   45m   Very Difficult
W. M. MacKenzie, A. M. MacAlpine, W. H. Murray and J. K. W. Dunn   Aug. 1936

From the ledge with the large slab leaning against the left wall, finish by the slabs on the left.

WINTER   IV
D. D. Stewart and W. M. Foster   March 1952

Start from the big bay on the left, to ascend the buttress trending right by snow ledges and short walls, crossing the ice wall on the original route at about 110m. Finish by easier climbing on the upper section of the buttress.

66   **Ordinary Route**   340m   Very Difficult
H. Raeburn   June 1902

Start well to the right of the lowest rocks, directly below the obvious chimney splitting the buttress higher up and just to the right of a projecting rib of rock.

Climb 10m to a small shelf and belay. Traverse up to the right, then back left to a large ledge, spike belay (21m). Climb to a large block belay in a square corner (18m). Move right, then up left to a corner with a flake belay high up on the wall (18m). Climb close to the chimney to a ledge with a large slab leaning against the left wall, thread belay (15m).

Climb the groove above, traverse right, then make an awkward step across the chimney to a large platform. Easier climbing leads to the broad ledge traversing the middle of the buttress. Finish by a square-cut buttress with giant steps, to reach the summit plateau close to the Observatory ruins. *Diagram page 62-63.*

WINTER   IV

J. R. Marshall and R. Smith   February 1960

A good climb with one hard section.

The lower rocks bank up well; steep snow with short ice steps is normally met on this section if the shallow depression in the centre of the buttress is followed. The upper chimney is often ice-choked and may present considerable difficulty. Above this section, a broad ledge is gained which can be traversed rightwards to escape into Observatory Gully. Continue up left to gain the crest of the buttress which is followed with minor difficulty to the plateau.

67   North-West Face   75m   IV

F. Craddock and C. Stead   March 1975

Further up the flank of the buttress on the right is a large bay with a chimney at the back which gives the route. It is short, sustained and may serve as an approach to the routes on the Indicator Wall above.

Start 25m right of the chimney and climb by steps up left to gain the icy upper groove. *Diagram page 62-63.*

INDICATOR WALL

This is the steep, slabby face above and to the right of the great ledge which girdles the Observatory Buttress. Defined on the left by the small gully of the Good Friday Climb, it extends right to terminate at the deep, narrow Gardyloo Gully.

68   Good Friday Climb   150m   III

G. G. MacPhee, R. W. Lovell, H. R. Shepherd and D. Edwards   April 1939

An enjoyable and popular route.

From the foot of Gardyloo Gully, traverse left along the easy terrace of Observatory Buttress to the foot of a narrow gully. Climb this on snow to a steep rock wall (60m). Traverse right on ice for 10m to a small gully. Climb up to the left on ice for 12m and continue upwards more easily for 45m to the foot of another small gully. Climb this for 15m, traverse right, then up in 12m to the plateau. *Diagram page 62-63.*

69   Indicator Wall   150m   V
T. King and G. Smith   February 1975

Start 45m right of the Good Friday Climb. Climb an iced chimney-groove right of a prominent spur, over ice bulges to a small snow scoop (30m). Climb fearsome bulge on the right and steep ice above, going up and right to the base of a short chimney-groove. Climb this and following bulge to snow slopes (45m). Continue by the gully for 45m to climb the steep headwall and cornice which is turned on the right. Belay on the indicator post. *Diagram page 62-63.*

70   Psychedelic Wall   180m   Very Severe
R. Marshall and J. R. Jackson   September 1967

A good, but dirty route. Start 18m left of Gardyloo Buttress, below a large detached flake.

Climb up to gain the flake from the right, then up and right to a ledge. Continue by the slabby arete on the left (peg runner) to ledge and belay (33m). Climb from the left by an arete to gain the left edge of a mossy ledge, peg belay (30m). Ascend the corner above for 3m, traverse left for 3m, then by a 6m wall to a ledge. Continue by the corner crack above to belay on top of an enormous block (21m). Climb grooves and cracks rightwards to a ledge beneath a prominent corner (25m). By the deep crack above, climb 6m to beneath a large block, move out right to climb by the right edge of a loose chimney to belay (27m). Gain good slabs, then finish by one of three corners in the final wall. Scramble to the plateau (45m). *Diagram page 62-63.*

WINTER   V

N. Muir and A. Paul   January 1978

Take a direct line, starting from the lowest rocks opposite the left edge of Gardyloo Buttress. Climb iced rocks to a snow bay (30m). Continue up steeper ice to gain a leftward trending snow ramp. From near the top of the ramp, take a groove leading to left edge of large plinth (45m). Continue by slabs to a corner (36m), then follow the corner and chimney above to below a steep wall (30m). Climb the rightmost of three corners, then mixed ground to negotiate a cornice finish.

N.B. Several other winter routes of similar standard have recently been climbed on this wall.

71 Observatory Gully 305m Easy

This gully, more in the nature of a small coire, separates the N.E. Buttress, Observatory Ridge and Observatory Buttress from the mass of Tower Ridge.

Starting as an easy scree slope, the gully gradually narrows and steepens to terminate beneath a high rock outcrop. On the left, the lower reaches of Gardyloo Gully breach this barrier and the rocks on its right are climbed to reach a broad terrace above. This terrace, continued left becomes the easy terrace of Observatory Buttress and, to the right, leads below Gardyloo Buttress, Tower Gully and extends to join the Eastern Traverse of Tower Ridge. In direct continuation above Observatory Gully is Gardyloo Gully. *Diagram page 62-63.*

WINTER   I

An uncomplicated snow ascent.

72 Gardyloo Gully 170m Severe

G. G. Macphee and R. C. Frost   August 1935

An old fashioned climb for the gully lover.

The gully is well defined; a number of short pitches lead to an awkward chockstone pitch, which is climbed by bridging. Easier climbing then leads under the great jammed boulder arch of the gully to the steep, final chimney. Climb the first 10m by bridging to a stance and runner and continue by the chimney, facing Gardyloo Buttress to good runners below the final capstone, 6m. A further 3m of chimney work with good holds under the roof lead awkwardly to the screes, below the plateau. The second should take precautions against stonefall, as there is much debris on this final section. *Diagram page 41 and 62-63.*

WINTER   II

G. Hastings and W. P. Haskett-Smith   April 1897

The difficulty of the climb depends on the amount and condition of the snow. Normally a uniform snow slope leads to a through route by a

F

tunnel of varying size, beyond which is a steep funnel. This is climbed by a short ice pitch, followed by steep snow which leads to the cornice which is sometimes difficult and often double.

If there is a great deal of snow, the through route and chockstone may be completely covered and the climb will then be a steep snow slope.

GARDYLOO BUTTRESS

The buttress dominates the exit narrows of Observatory Gully and consists of two ridges, of which the left hand is fairly well defined, with a shallow depression between them. The upper part of this depression opens out into a wide funnel with what is almost a gully at the back. Water from this gully drains down over two long, steep, smooth grooves slanting down from left to right.

73   Left Edge Route   155m   Very Severe
J. R. Marshall, G. J. Ritchie and R. Marshall   June 1962

A superb route with fine situations.

Start at the lowest left hand point of the buttress at the foot of Gardyloo Gully.

Climb the crest above by awkward tilting grooves to belay by an old peg (28m). Gain the slab above, turn a rib on the right, then climb directly to belay beneath a crack and flake (18m). Climb the crack, move up right past an old peg, mantelshelf a sloping ledge, then round a rib on the right to enter a shallow groove. Climb this 3m, move right to gain the left edge of a slab and follow the edge to belays (30m). Continue up the edge for 3m, traverse horizontally right to a groove which is climbed for 2m until a crack leads back left to the crest and belays (30m). Follow the crest by steep walls and steps to the plateau (30m and 15m). *Diagram page 62-63.*

WINTER   V
R. Carrington and A. Rouse   March 1976

This route requires a good plating of snow and ice. The summer route is followed with a peg for tension to gain the upper slab section.

10 Gardyloo Buttress, pitch one (Ken Crocket).   *Photo: C. Gilmore*

74   Kellett's Route   138m   Very Severe

B. P. Kellett   July 1944

A good climb.

Start 25m right of the lowest rocks.

Climb easily to the foot of a corner (25m). Climb the left wall by cracks to a belay (12m). Traverse right below an overhang, then climb a bulge to gain a recess. Climb the corner with difficulty to reach easier rocks under three parallel grooves (43m). Climb into the right hand groove and follow this to a stance and belay below a right-angled corner (21m). Climb the corner, move left to climb an easier corner leading into the lower rocks of the upper gully (12m). Follow this with little difficulty to finish (25m). *Diagram page 62-63.*

VARIATION   62m   Severe

D. Haston and J. Stenhouse   September 1958

Leave the final gully bed at its lowest point to climb the left-hand ridge in two pitches of 35m and 27m.

75   Smith's Route   125m   V

R. Smith and J. R. Marshall   February 1960

A short, sustained modern classic with poor belays.

Start directly below the lower end of the slanting grooves.

Climb a snow and ice groove for 35m to the foot of the main grooves, peg belay. Traverse up and left across the lower groove to easier climbing, turn up to a steepening, break out and up right on steep ice to gain the left edge of the upper slab groove, which is climbed to the foot of the upper funnel (45m). Continue by the funnel to the plateau. A good plating of snow ice is recommended for this climb. *Diagram page 62-63.*

VARIATION

Normally a great icicle forms above the first stance. If this is sufficiently established, climb it to enter the groove directly from an indifferent belay in a cave above the first stance of the original route. This is the most popular way.

76 Tower Gully 110m I

G. Hastings, E. L. W. Haskett-Smith and W. P. Haskett-Smith April 1897

This gully defines the right, or west flank of Gardyloo Buttress, starting from the easy slope above the rock barrier in Observatory Gully. It is gained by a right traverse from the top of Observatory Gully, above the rock barrier.

The gully is an uncomplicated snow slope with a dangerous outrun and sometimes a large cornice. *Diagram page 41 and 62-63.*

TOWER RIDGE, EAST FLANK

The following routes all ascend the eastern, or left flank of the Tower Ridge.

77 Tower Scoop 65m III

I. S. Clough and G. Grandison January 1961

Start under the rock barrier which terminates Observatory Gully at a point midway between the lower reaches of Gardyloo Gully and a deep cleft close to the very steep flank of Tower Ridge.

Climb an ice pitch to gain the scoop above; climb this, finishing by an awkward corner and snow funnel to gain the terrace above, directly below Tower Gully. *Diagram page 78.*

78 Tower Cleft 75m III

G. Pratt and J. Francis February 1949

This route follows the deep cleft in the angle formed by the rock barrier containing Tower Scoop and the flank of Tower Ridge. *Diagram page 78.*

79 Rolling Stones 135m Very Severe

J. Cunningham and C. Higgins August 1965

Start 30m right of Tower Cleft

Climb easily to rock shelves and belay (25m). Traverse horizontally right by a good rock ledge beneath an overhanging wall. Climb a broken wall at the end of the traverse to reach a large ledge and belay (12m). From the right end of the ledge, traverse 18m to an overhanging recess 1.5m wide; climb this to gain a small ledge on the left, peg belay (25m). Climb the corner above, traverse right to reach a wide crack, then climb to a good belay (43m). Continue by easier rock to reach the foot of the Great Tower (30m). *Diagram page 78.*

11 Tower Ridge, Eastern Traverse (Ken Crocket). *Photo: C. Gilmore*

80   Echo Traverse   135m   IV

J. R. Marshall and R. Marshall   February 1966

Start a little right of Tower Cleft and climb snow and ice slopes to a large ledge under the steep upper wall (60m). Traverse easily rightwards to the base of a chimney recess. (The traverse can be continued on to the crest of Tower Ridge as East Wall Route, II). Start up a groove left of the chimney to a large spike belay (6m). Traverse the slab on the left (hard under thin conditions) then up by a short chimney-groove to gain a snow bay. Continue by the left-trending fault above, in two pitches to the crest of the ridge, just under the Great Tower. *Diagram page 78.*

81   The Brass Monkey   130m   Hard Very Severe

J. R. Marshall and J. Stenhouse   May 1961

This route follows the deep crack in the corner formed by the great projection of Echo Wall, at a point halfway up Observatory Gully. It gives a good climb.

Climb to the slab apex beneath the corner (65m). Move up the corner for 3m, traverse right to gain the base of the crack (aid used on original ascent). Follow the crack in three pitches to the crest of Tower Ridge (65m). *Diagram page 78.*

82   The Great Chimney   65m   Severe

G.G. Macphee and A. G. Murray   September 1935

75m north of Echo Wall, a conspicuous, deeply cut chimney cleaves the flank of Tower Ridge. A large chockstone jammed far out is a useful identification characteristic. The rock scenery within the chimney is impressive.

Scramble to the foot of the chimney (75m). Climb 6m to a recess, then 15m to belays and a small chockstone. Loose rock leads in 6m to a vertical block with cracks on each side. Climb the left crack on good holds within and, using sloping footholds high on the left wall, gain easier climbing and a stance (8m). From this point, a restricted through route, or an outside route can be followed to finish at a narrow saddle on the crest of Tower Ridge below the Little Tower. *Diagram page 78.*

WINTER   IV

J. R. Marshall and R. Smith   February 1960

Follow the summer line.

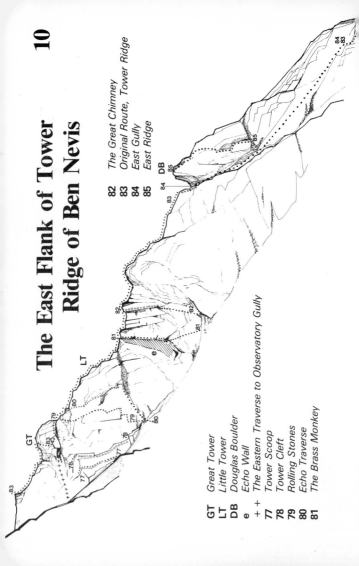

The East Flank of Tower Ridge of Ben Nevis

10

82 The Great Chimney
83 Original Route, Tower Ridge
84 East Gully
85 East Ridge

GT Great Tower
LT Little Tower
DB Douglas Boulder
e Echo Wall
+ + The Eastern Traverse to Observatory Gully
77 Tower Scoop
78 Tower Cleft
79 Rolling Stones
80 Echo Traverse
81 The Brass Monkey

TOWER RIDGE

One of the best known names on the mountain, it is the second of the great buttresses of Ben Nevis and projects far northwards from the precipice, to separate Observatory Gully on the east, from the open, scenic Coire na Ciste to the west.

A short distance above the C.I.C. Hut, the ridge rises from the glen at a level of 701m and sweeps some 215m to the top of the Douglas Boulder, an imposing rock pinnacle separated from the main ridge by a deep cleft—the Douglas Gap. Above this gap, the ridge narrows and after an almost level section, rises over two major steps until the ridge is barred by the precipitous Great Tower. From the large cairn on its summit at over 1,220m, a short descent leads to the Tower Gap, from which easy rocks lead to the summit plateau at a height of 1,340m.

There is one main route with variations and numerous subsidiary routes which attain the crest of the ridge by the steep, varied east and west flanks.

83   Original Route   610m   Difficult
J., E., and B. Hopkinson   September 1892

The ordinary route is described first. Strictly speaking, the Douglas Boulder should be included as the first part of the climb. If this is not done, turn the Douglas Boulder on the east side and climb the rocks above a grassy bay to reach an ill-defined hollow, then by the narrow East Gully to the Douglas Gap. It is easy to miss the lower section in mist, but a useful guide is the grassy bay.

A metre to the east of the highest part of the gap, an 18m chimney leads to the crest of the ridge, which is quite narrow and almost level, but soon steepens to the first step, an overhanging wall which is climbed to and turned by a ledge slanting to the right. Above this, moderate scrambling leads by a series of rises to another almost level section. Two indentations are crossed here; on the left of the second is the top of the Great Chimney. Beyond the second cleft is the base of the Little Tower. The route is by the rocks on the left edge until an awkward ledge can be followed rightwards to a corner. It is possible to climb straight up the face.

Here it can be seen that the Little Tower is in reality the second step of the ridge.

Easy rocks now lead by the crest and should be followed to the very ramparts of the Great Tower under its north-eastern corner. To the east, or left, a level grassy ledge, the Eastern Traverse is followed, to cross an exposed but easy groove, then round some rocks to enter the foot of a tunnel formed by a huge, fallen block. From the top of this through route, a few metres more lead to steep, but easy rocks on the right which are climbed straight up on good holds to the summit of the Great Tower, cairn. (The continuation of the Eastern Traverse may be followed easily all the way to the top of Observatory Gully, making a useful escape route.) From the top of the Tower, a slight descent is made to traverse a narrow crest leading to the Tower Gap, where the situation is quite exposed, but the steep rocks on the far side have good holds to facilitate the crossing. Easier rocks then lead to a final steepening which is turned on the right by a ledge and groove to reach the summit plateau. *Diagram page 41 and 78.*

WINTER   III

J. N. Collie, G. A. Solly and J. Collier   March 1894

‘ In winter the Tower Ridge provides one of the finest mountaineering expeditions in these islands. Depending on conditions, all degrees of difficulty may be encountered and the ridge has been known to baffle experienced parties.

To anyone knowing the configuration of the ridge in summer, it should always be possible, given time, to force an ascent; but unless the ground is familiar it would be unwise to push the climb under bad conditions. Time being an important factor on a short winter's day, it is better to beat an orderly retreat than spend an involuntary night out. In this connection, the easy escape route by following the Eastern Traverse to Observatory Gully will save many unwitting bivouacs at the foot of the Great Tower.

GREAT TOWER VARIATIONS

BELL'S ROUTE   45m   Very Difficult

J. H. B. Bell and E. E. Roberts   August 1929

From the crest of the ridge at the foot of the north-east arete, climb a slab, then traverse up, on good holds across the northern face of the Tower making for the obvious block on the right. A difficult stride has to be made before the crack and the top of the block can be gained (18m). Climb the steep scoop above on good holds to the top of the Tower.

RECESS ROUTE   45m   Difficult
W. W. Naismith and G. Thomson   September 1894

From the foot of the north-west arete of the Tower, climb up to a broad platform at 5m. A chimney recess is visible 6m above; climb from a large block into the recess (thread belay on the right). Continue above the belay on good holds to the top of the Tower.

THE DOUGLAS BOULDER

The following routes ascend the rocks of the Douglas Boulder.

84   **East Gully**   155m   Easy

This is the gully followed to the Douglas Gap on the Original route. It gives easy scrambling. *Diagram page 78.*

WINTER   I

A straightforward snow ascent, but with a dangerous outrun.

85   **East Ridge**   65m   Difficult
J. H. Bell and R. G. Napier   April 1896

Climb as for the Original Route to the point where the East Gully begins to be defined. A large grass ledge leads to the right; traverse this for 10m, then climb steep, but easy rock to belay in a square corner (27m). Climb this and a similar corner above in two pitches of 6m. Easier rocks lead to the top of the Boulder (18m). *Diagram page 78.*

86   **Direct Route**   215m   Very Difficult
W. Brown, L. Hinxman, H. Raeburn and W. Douglas   April 1896

Start at the lowest rocks, a little left of a smooth slab wall which is an obvious feature of the lower section of the face.

Climb easily by a shallow groove for 45m to a point where the groove steepens to form an open chimney. Climb this for 60m to gain a well-defined ledge. Traverse this to the right and climb steep, broken rock to the top of the Boulder. *Diagram page 83.*

WINTER   IV

Climb as for summer with the chimney providing considerable difficulty, particularly under light cover. An interesting climb.

87   Direct Route II   215m   Severe
D. Browning and H. Small   Summer 1967

A pleasant route on good rock. Start under the right edge of the smooth slab wall which is a prominent characteristic of the lower rocks of the Boulder.

Climb the slab just right of a sickle scoop to the terrace above; scramble to the foot of the steep upper section which is climbed direct. The crux is at the top of the wall where easier rock is gained from the top of a leaning block. Continue more easily to the top of the Boulder. *Diagram page 83.*

88   North-West Face   215m   Difficult
W. G. McClymont and J. H. B. Bell   May 1936

Good rock and climbing, especially in the central section. As viewed from the hut, a feature of the north-west face are three chimneys in the form of an inverted "N". The route is climbed to the base of these, then follows the central chimney.

Start to the right of the prominent, smooth slab wall of the lower rocks.

Climb an easy-angled groove to a short wall barring access to the left-hand chimney (45m). Climb the wall to enter the chimney (6m). Follow the chimney 6m, then traverse slabs rightwards to gain the central, diagonal chimney (18m). Follow the chimney to its final section which narrows and contains a chockstone. Some 6m below this chockstone, traverse slabs to the rib on the right, then climb up and left to finish at the chimney exit (25m). A choice of routes then lead to the top of the Boulder. *Diagram page 83.*

89   Left Hand Chimney   215m   Difficult
B. P. Kellett   June 1944

Start as for the North-West Face and climb to the base of the left-hand chimney. The chimney is continued beyond the point where that route traverses into the central chimney. Climb a series of short pitches to reach a large ledge. The line of the chimney is continued above and is followed to the summit of the Boulder. *Diagram page 83.*

The Douglas Boulder of Ben Nevis

11

86   *Direct Route*
87   *Direct Route II*
88   *North-West Face*
89   *Left Hand Chimney*
90   *Cutlass*
91   *South-West Ridge*

WINTER   IV

R. Carrington and J. R. Marshall   February 1972

Start by a long traverse over snow from the lowest rocks on the left. A short vertical wall is climbed to gain the chimney which provides sustained difficulties.

90 Cutlass   145m   Very Severe

E. Cairns and F. Harper   July 1963

This enjoyable climb follows the clean-cut corner which lies some 30m left of the South-West Ridge of the Douglas Boulder.

Climb by easy slabs 40m to a flake belay. Move up into the corner, belay (9m). Climb the corner to a ledge and belay on the right wall (30m). Continue by the chimney above in two pitches to gain the South-West Ridge (45m). *Diagram page 83 and 89.*

91 South-West Ridge   180m   Moderate

J. W. Burns, W. A. Morrison, W. C. Newbigging and A. E. Robertson   Aug. 1904

The route follows the crest of the well-defined ridge overlooking West Gully and is the easiest of the face routes to the top of the Douglas Boulder. It gives good situations, but on shattered rock. *Diagram page 83 and 89.*

WINTER   III

J. Y. MacDonald and H. W. Turnbull   March 1934

An interesting climb, by the summer route.

92 West Gully   140m   Easy

The West Gully leads to the Douglas Gap and, while slightly steeper, it is more direct than the East Gully when approaching from the C.I.C. Hut. *Diagram page 89.*

WINTER   I

The gully is a straightforward ascent on snow. The traverse of the Gap, i.e. up West Gully and down East Gully, provides an interesting expedition.

SECONDARY TOWER RIDGE

This lies on the west flank of Tower Ridge and some distance below its crest, taking the form of a slanting shelf, parallel to the main ridge and separated from it by a well-defined depression which holds snow until late in the season.

For the most part, it hardly attains the status of a distinct ridge. At its upper extremity it rises steeply to the top of the Pinnacle Buttress of the Tower, to terminate just below and to the west of the Great Tower.

93   1934 Route   185m   Moderate

Start 45m right of West Gully. Climb by a wide, shallow gully for 45m, then traverse right into a slabby groove which is climbed for 45m, followed by scrambling to reach a point above Vanishing Gully. Follow the crest for 100m, then traverse left to gain the crest of Tower Ridge below the Little Tower. *Diagram page 89.*

WINTER   II

J. Y. MacDonald and H. W. Turnbull   March 1934

Climb snow to the slabby groove which often holds ice and presents the only real difficulty. Then follow the snow shelf to the upper reaches of Tower Ridge where a choice of routes, up or down may be made.

94   1931 Route   125m   Difficult

J. Y. MacDonald and H. W. Turnbull   March 1931

Some 90m further along the west flank of Tower Ridge in a bay formed by a steep, projecting buttress, twin chimneys lead up to the crest of the Secondary Tower Ridge. The 1931 Route uses the right hand of these.

Climb to a belay on the left wall (8m). Continue up the chimney under a chockstone, generally using the left wall to reach a platform at 18m. The chimney now opens out to become a groove and this is followed with little difficulty in three pitches to reach the 1934 Route which is then crossed to gain the shallow gully dividing the Secondary Tower Ridge from the Tower Ridge. *Diagram page 89.*

WINTER   III

G. Wallace and R. Shaw   January 1961

Climb steep snow into the chimney which is then followed over three short pitches to reach the easier upper snows of the 1934 Route. A choice of routes up or down may then be taken.

VARIATION   50m   Difficult

B. P. Kellett   June 1943

Follow the left of the twin chimneys to join the groove of the 1934 Route.

95   Vagabond's Rib   200m   Severe

I. S. Clough   April 1959

A pleasant climb.

Start 65m right of the West Gully, directly below steep slabs bounded on the right by a hanging gully (Vanishing Gully).

Climb easily to a belay centrally placed below the slab (15m). Climb the slab to a niche and belay (24m). Move out right and climb the steep crest by a groove and crack to belays (18m). Continue more easily by the slabs ahead to reach the crest of Tower Ridge in 90m. *Diagram page 89.*

96   Vanishing Gully   200m   V

R. Marshall and G. Tiso   January 1961

This is the conspicuous gully which drains the lower part of the Secondary Tower Ridge. The top part is deep and wide, but lower down it narrows to a crack and finally disappears.

Under normal conditions the gully presents an ice fall over the lower 65m. It is a superb climb with good belays and protection.

Climb mixed snow and ice to the ice fall, then by steep ice to an ice cave at 12m on a narrow, horizontal ledge. This provides a magnificent belay, but can be buried. Continue by a bulging ice wall, past a mid-way cave which can also be buried, to easier ground (18m). Climb another steep ice pitch, then left to the easier upper reaches and a junction with the Secondary Tower Ridge. *Diagram page 89.*

97   Rogue's Rib   215m   Severe

T. W. Patey and J. Smith   April 1956

A less interesting climb than its appearance would suggest.

This is the name given to the steep, two-tiered buttress which projects from the west flank of Tower Ridge, just beyond the chimneys of the 1934 Route. On the first ascent, the steep lower pitches were avoided by the gully on the right which was then snow filled. Shortly after,

12 Vanishing Gully.

Photo: A. Kimber

K. Bryan and N. Harthill ascended from the lowest rocks and continued by the original line to make the first complete ascent.

Start immediately left of the Italian Climb, the gully which bounds the buttress on the right.

Climb the crest to belay (21m), then by the right flank to a large platform (30m). Continue up the shallow chimney above for 27m to gain easier climbing which leads in 65m to the base of the upper tier of the buttress. Climb by thin cracks for 10m, then traverse left into the obvious chimney to belay (18m). Follow the chimney to some huge, perched blocks, traverse right, climb up behind a large flake to reach a chockstone belay (24m). Continue by the chimney above, or the ridge on the right to the top of the buttress (30m). *Diagram page 89.*

WINTER   IV

I. S. Clough and G. Grandison   January 1960

Climb as for the original ascent, using the lower section of the Italian Climb, then by cracks and grooves to the top of the buttress.

98   **The Italian Climb**   180m   III

J. R. Marshall, A. McCorquodale and G. J. Ritchie   January 1958

This is the name given to the deep-cut gully which defines the right flank of the buttress of Rogue's Rib. The gully starts abruptly.

The first chimney presents an ice groove leading into a cave, the exit from which is difficult. Snow then leads to the upper chimney which gives a steep ice pitch some 10m high with normally the rock projecting to allow bridging up over the cave. The upper section of the gully trends right at an easier angle by snow slopes and occasional ice to the crest of Tower Ridge. When well banked up, the lower pitches are reduced to short ice walls. *Diagram page 89.*

VARIATION   IV

S. Belk and I. Fulton

An improvement to the original line, but harder. Climb the ice fall on the right wall of the lower section of the climb and rejoin the easier upper part.

12
The West Flank of Tower Ridge of Ben Nevis

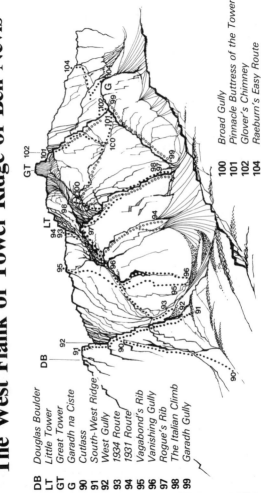

DB Douglas Boulder
LT Little Tower
GT Great Tower
G Garadh na Ciste
90 Cutlass
91 South-West Ridge
92 West Gully
93 1934 Route
94 1931 Route
95 Vagabond's Rib
96 Vanishing Gully
97 Rogue's Rib
98 The Italian Climb
99 Garadh Gully

100 Broad Gully
101 Pinnacle Buttress of the Tower
102 Glover's Chimney
104 Raeburn's Easy Route

GARADH NA CISTE

Beyond Italian Climb, the main flank of Tower Ridge is separated from Coire na Ciste by a deeply-cut gully, Garadh Gully. To the right of the gully is a small buttress crowned by a spacious platform. This is Garadh na Ciste, so named from its resemblance to a "Jardin" in the Alps.

99 Garadh Gully 95m II
I. S. Clough and M. Bucke February 1958

This is the deep gully which leads from the foot of Italian Climb to Garadh na Ciste.

Under normal conditions the gully gives a straightforward climb with two short, steep ice pitches, each of 15m. Later in the season, it may bank out to a uniform snow slope. The gully can usefully be linked to other routes starting higher on the flank of Tower Ridge. *Diagram page 89.*

100 Broad Gully 95m Easy
B. P. Kellett July 1943

From the top of Garadh na Ciste, a raking scree gully leads up left across the face, under the Pinnacle Buttress to join the Secondary Tower Ridge. Continue beyond this with little difficulty, to gain the crest of Tower Ridge, just below the Little Tower. *Diagram page 89.*

WINTER II
I. S. Clough and M. Bucke February 1958

The summer route is followed to Tower Ridge and is useful as a line of descent from the lower lines on Secondary Tower Ridge.

101 Pinnacle Buttress of the Tower 150m Difficult
G. T. Glover and W. Inglis Clark June 1902

Start about 45m up Broad Gully. Climb a corner and crack, steep, but with good holds (21m). Easier ground trending up right leads to a broad ledge (18m). This, if followed continues into Tower Gap West Chimney, however leave the ledge under the steep upper prow of the buttress to climb by a rightward raking groove (30m). Move up left by a

chimney groove to reach a ledge above the prow of the buttress (12m).
Traverse left into a groove leading through slabs to easier ground (30m).
Now follow the crest of the ridge to the foot of the Great Tower (30m).

The above description probably gives the best line of ascent, but
many variations are possible, both left and right of the crest of the
buttress. *Diagram page 89.*

WINTER   III/IV

D. J. Bennet and A. Tait   November 1957

The ascent went by the rocks to the right of the buttress. From the top
of the Garadh na Ciste, follow Broad Gully until a ledge can be taken,
raking up rightwards for some 75m to a point a little beyond the steep
crest of the upper section of the buttress. Climb by a snow filled groove
(18m). Traverse right for 12m to another groove which is followed to
easier rocks leading left on to the top of the buttress below the Great
Tower. A selection of routes lead to the plateau (see Tower Ridge).
Route finding on the lower section can be difficult.

102   Glover's Chimney (Tower Gap West Chimney)   140m
Very Difficult

G. T. Glover and Dr and Mrs Inglis Clark   June 1902

The climb starts from the Garadh na Ciste and goes directly by the
narrow gully to the Tower Gap. The lowest rocks are overhanging and
normally wet.

Climb a short distance by an ill-defined ledge which rakes steeply up
right and gain the right wall. Surmount a short, steep section of rather
smooth rock then, by a traverse left, regain the gully bed 60m above the
start. Continue up the gully by short, easy pitches to the final chimney
which is climbed by bridging well out, to finish on the right, or by
climbing the chimney direct (harder). *Diagram page 89.*

WINTER   III

G. G. Macphee, G. C. Williams and D. Henderson   March 1935

This is a very fine and popular route.

Under normal conditions the lower rocks are masked by a great ice
fall, which involves 30m on steep ice, followed by 10m of snow to gain a
stance. Mixed snow and ice lead back left into the gully which is
followed, mainly on snow to the final chimney. This can be climbed by
the right or left walls or directly to the Tower Gap.

103 Goodeve's Route   140m   III

T. E. Goodeve, C. Inglis Clark and J. H. A. McIntyre   December 1907

This climb was the result of a successful attempt by a belated party to escape off Tower Ridge. After a descent from the Western Traverse (under the Great Tower), down Glover's Chimney, they baulked at the ice fall and took to the rocks on the right to make their epic escape to the plateau.

If started independently as described below, the route provides an excellent winter climb, which comes into condition early and remains so throughout the season.

Climb the initial icefall of Glover's Chimney, or another icefall to the right, cross a snow ramp and continue just right of the chimney to gain a snow ledge leading up right. Climb an icefall, difficult to start, to reach a snowfield, from the top of which climb a short chimney, then a shallow gully to open snow slopes, to finish at the same point as Tower Ridge. Variation is possible. Not shown on diagram.

104 Raeburn's Easy Route   110m   Easy

H. Raeburn and A. W. Russell   September 1911

This gives a scenic scramble.

Start above and right of Garadh na Ciste, about 60m left of Number Two Gully.

Traverse up to the left until an easy staircase leads to a ledge sloping up right for a short distance. Easy scrambling leads left again to a wide, sloping ledge below the final steep wall. Follow the ledge right for a considerable distance to finish up a well-defined gully giving access to the summit plateau midway between the top of Number Two Gully and Tower Ridge. *Diagram page 89 and 96-97.*

WINTER   II

S. M. C. Party   April 1920

A thick mantle of snow and ice completely alters the character of this climb.

From near the foot of Number Two Gully, traverse left under a steep wall to a large icefall. Climb this for 30m to gain a snow slope leading to a long right traverse below the final wall, which is turned by steep snow at the far end. Gain the plateau by the easiest route over the cornice which is not usually heavy at this point.

NUMBER TWO GULLY BUTTRESS

Beyond the rather indeterminate wall of Raeburn's Easy Route is a scimitar shaped buttress, defined on the right by the deeply cut Number Two Gully. This is Number Two Gully Buttress. Its lower third is set at a low angle, with only the upper section giving continuous climbing.

105 WINTER   120m   III
J. R. Marshall, L. S. Lovat and A. H. Hendry   March 1958

An enjoyable short route.

Mixed rock and ice at an easy angle lead to a large snow field under the steepening of the buttress. About 18m left of the crest of the buttress, climb a steep ice groove for 21m, then by mixed snow and ice trend right to reach the crest of the buttress a little below the plateau. *Diagram page 96-97.*

VARIATION   III
I. S. Clough, N. Stebbing, P. Cresswell, W. Reid, N. Bull and D. Ducker   April 1960

After the easier section, climb by a groove line just left of the crest, then by the crest to the plateau. This is generally a more difficult line.

Hard short routes may be made to the left of these routes.

106 **Number Two Gully**   120m   II
J. Collier, G. Hastings and W. C. Slingsby   Easter 1896

A pleasant route passing through good scenery.

The gully fills up well and normally presents a steep snow slope with sometimes a short ice pitch at the narrows. The cornice is occasionally large and difficult. *Diagram page 41 and 96-97.*

COMB GULLY BUTTRESS

This is the wedge-shaped buttress to the right of Number Two Gully. A narrow, easy angled crest leads to the broad middle section topped by a steep rampart. The right flank is defined by the narrow, twisting Comb Gully.

107 WINTER 125m III/IV

I. S. Clough and J. M. Alexander January 1960

Climb just left of the lower rocks, or gain the central snow field from Number Two Gully. Follow a groove on the left edge of the buttress, then make a traverse rising right to the foot of a prominent, curving chimney in the steep, final rocks. Climb the chimney, then trend left to the plateau. The chimney is rarely in condition and the variation next described is more often climbed. It gives an interesting climb with a sting in the tail. *Diagram page 96-97.*

VARIATION 75m IV

I. Fulton and D. Gardner January 1971

After the groove on the ordinary route, avoid the right traverse and go left to below an ice column, which is climbed to gain an ice filled groove. Follow this groove which narrows and steepens to its top.

108 **Comb Gully** 125m III/IV

F. G. Stangle, R. Morsley and P. A. Small April 1938

A splendid and popular climb which is in condition for much of the winter. It bounds Comb Gully Buttress on its right.

Climb steep snow to the upper section. This gives four ice pitches of increasing difficulty. The first is climbed by the left wall, the middle ones by bridging and the final one on the right wall by an awkward bulge. Under heavy snow it may bank out to give a much easier climb. *Diagram page 96-97.*

COMB BUTTRESS (THE COMB)

This buttress dominates the southerly part of Coire na Ciste as a great wedge, girdled at one third height by a raking ledge rising from left to right. On each flank, steep gullies define the buttress; to the east Comb Gully and to the west or right Green Gully, which separates the Comb from Number Three Gully Buttress. Below the raking ledge the buttress is easy angled and slabby, whereas the upper tier is protected for most of its length on the northern side by considerable overhangs, forcing recorded lines of ascent on to the eastern and western flanks of the buttress.

109 **Tower Face of the Comb**   215m   V
R. Smith and R. Holt   January 1959

From the left end of the raking ledge which splits the buttress about one third height, move up 30m to the highest of the ledges which run parallel to the main ledge.

Traverse the ledge rightwards to near its termination (25m). Climb the obvious groove above, turn a steepening on the left to gain easier climbing (18m). Climb more easily to the base of a steep wall (50m). Traverse right over steep snow and short walls to reach the buttress edge. The crest of the buttress, although easier can take much time, particularly in high wind or deep powder snow. *Diagram page 96-97.*

This is a sustained climb on difficult mixed ground.

110 **Pigott's Route**   245m   Severe
A. S. Pigott and J. Wilding   September 1921

This is an old-fashioned classic.

Start at the lowest point on the northerly side of the buttress.

Climb by a chimney for 24m, then easy rocks to gain the raking ledge 60m above the start. Follow the ledge right to near its termination in Green Gully, to a point just beyond a large block. Climb the undercut flake chimney to reach a grass stance and belay (10m). Continue directly by steep slabs and ribs to a grass ledge (21m). Easier climbing leads to the crest of the buttress which is followed with fine situations to the summit plateau. *Diagram page 96-97.*

WINTER   IV
J. R. Marshall and R. Smith   February 1960

The lower section is avoided and the raking ledge followed on snow to the base of the flake chimney which is climbed with difficulty. Above, a left traverse is made for 10m to gain a steep ice-filled groove leading to the buttress crest.

This is another sustained climb on mixed ground.

111 **Green Gully**   125m   III/IV
H. Raeburn and E. Phildius   April 1906

This is the gully which separates Comb Buttress from the broad Number Three Gully Buttress on its right. More in the form of a groove

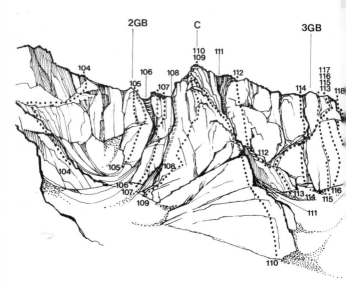

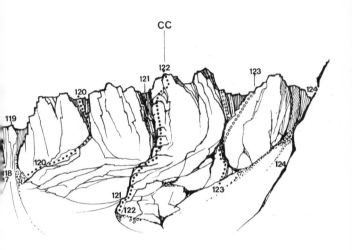

than a gully, it can generally be relied on to be in climbable condition
throughout most winters.

It is a fine companion route to Comb Gully and its first ascent was a
remarkable achievement for its day.

The lower rocks are masked by a steep banking of snow from which a
steep 12m wall of ice leads to the easy ground of the traverse ledge.
Above, two short ice pitches lead to another ice pitch some 18m high;
this sometimes presents an awkward ice bulge best climbed from right to
left. Snow then leads to the final difficulties which can present another
steep pitch, bulging in its upper reaches.

The climb lacks protection. *Diagram page 96-97.*

NUMBER THREE GULLY BUTTRESS

Adjoining Green Gully on its left, a slab wall extends to abut the main
mass of the buttress which presents a steep, impressive face overlooking
Lochan na Ciste and Number Three Gully further to the right.

112 Aphrodite 180m III/IV
M. G. Geddes and J. C. Higham March 1971

This route climbs the left side of the buttress.

Start up the same snow depression as the Original Route (see below),
but from the top of the depression move up left, mainly by snow ledges
until possible to move down slightly to gain the foot of an open groove.
This groove lies just right of the rib beside Green Gully and is undercut
by a large rock wall. Climb the groove and its continuation on the crest
to the right of Green Gully (peg on first ascent). Move up right across
snow to surmount the cornice. *Diagram page 96-97.*

113 Original Route 125m Moderate
H. Raeburn and Dr and Mrs Inglis Clark June 1903

This good route starts up the easy rocks to the right of Green Gully to
gain the foot of a long groove raking up to the right (24m). Follow the
groove for 45m to reach a large corner, above which a steep chimney-
crack rises. Traverse right, then up by steep, but easy rocks to arrive at a
large platform (6m). Climb up to a smaller platform (6m). Traverse
rightwards to gain an obvious ledge leading across the upper face of the
buttress (30m). From the end of the ledge, climb by slabby rock to the
plateau (6m). *Diagram page 96-97.*

VARIATION   35m   Very Difficult

From the smaller platform, climb up to the left to belay near the foot of a well-defined chimney (15m). Climb the steep chimney, exposed, with loose rock in the lower part then, by a recess above, climb to the plateau.

WINTER   III

L. S. Lovat and D. Bennet   February 1957

This is an excellent short route.

Climb to gain a snow shelf raking up to the right, then from the highest point, traverse right by steep ice and snow to gain the large platform. If the chimney variant is followed as on the first ascent, climb steep ice in two pitches of 10m and 12m to finish. If the summer line is followed, climb to gain the obvious traverse ledge leading across the face and follow this to a stance at the far end. An iced slab leads to the top.

Both these lines of ascent are in exposed positions.

114   **Two-Step Corner**   125m   IV

D. Kirtley and D. Montgomery   March 1975

Left of the steep front of the buttress is a large corner broken by the traverse line of the Original Route. This is the line of the route.

Start right of the Original Route and climb the corner to belay on the traverse ledge. Continue by the corner above, now very steep to the plateau. The cornice may be difficult. *Diagram page 96-97.*

115   **The Knuckleduster**   125m   Hard Very Severe

J. R. Marshall and R. Marshall   September 1966

This very fine route ascends the great groove which is an obvious feature of the steep face of the buttress overlooking Lochan na Ciste.

Climb the groove to belay under the overhang (40m). Continue, turning the overhang by a slab on the right, belay on the outer edge (15m). Regain the groove by a horizontal ledge, continue by a crack in the right wall to belay (36m). Climb the wall on the right to gain the large platform of the Original Route (30m). *Diagram page 96-97.*

116 **Sioux Wall**   125m   Hard Very Severe

I. B. Nicholson and G. Grassam   September 1972

An excellent route on good rock.

This lies on the steep face of the buttress to the right of Knuckleduster and starts below the obvious large groove of that route.

Follow a diagonal weakness up and right to beneath grooves in the centre of the face (40m). Climb the wall to a crack, then move left onto a ramp which is followed to a ledge at the start of the grooves. Continue by the groove, moving left at a roof to a peg belay (40m). Climb the steep crack and groove above to surmount easily a small overhang to a belay (24m). Climb directly to finish. *Diagram page 96-97.*

117 **Thompson's Route**   110m   III

R. Marshall, J. R. Marshall and J. Stenhouse   December 1963

A good climb, less often in condition than the Original Route.

Start from the foot of Number Three Gully and follow the chimney bounding the right flank of the very steep front of the buttress to the large platform of the Original Route. Finish by an iced corner just right of the variant chimneys. *Diagram page 96-97.*

118 **Gargoyle Wall**   125m   Very Difficult

W. Peascod, B. L. Dodson, C. Peckett, J. Renwick and G. G. Macphee   Aug. 1950

The Gargoyle is well seen on the right skyline from the descent of Number Three Gully. Start 10m right of the Chimney of Thompson's Route on the ledge which cuts across the top of the first pitch.

Climb the steep wall above by a zigzag route to a well-defined ledge (31m). Descend slightly from the left end of the ledge to enter the first chimney which is climbed, surmounting a large chockstone to gain a rocky bay level with the Gargoyle, now visible on the right (31m). Traverse to the Gargoyle, crossing a groove, then a short gangway on to the head (10m). Climb the ridge above, past a perched block to a ledge, traverse right into a corner and belay (12m). Climb the corner to stance and block belay below a steep wall (6m). Continue by the steep crack above to a rock platform and belays (10m). Traverse 6m left to a chimney crack which is climbed on good holds to a stance and belay (18m). Climb the chimney with more difficulty (6m). (This section can be avoided on the left.) The continuation of the chimney is followed more easily to the top in 6m. *Diagram page 96-97.*

WINTER   IV

R. Carrington and I. Nicholson   December 1977

Climb the iced chimney of Thompson's Route and traverse right onto the Gargoyle. Then, follow the summer route with difficulty on the upper cracks.

NUMBER THREE GULLY

This gully is situated centrally at the back of Coire na Ciste and separates Number Three Gully Buttress from Creag Coire na Ciste. The gully is easily identified by a pinnacle standing as a flat-topped blade of rock at the head of the gully. This feature is a useful summer aid to the recognition of the gully in mist. The descent of the gully should be started from the left or west of this pinnacle.

119   **Original Route**   90m   Easy

Climbed circa 1870, it is a straightforward ascent on scree with a loose scramble of 10m to finish. *Diagram page 41 and 96-97.*

WINTER   I

J. N. Collie and W. Travers   Easter 1895

In winter a uniform snow slope fills the gully. The cornice can be large, but there is normally an easy break to the right of the pinnacle.

The gully is much used as a quick descent. After the first 10m, which are often icy, it provides an easy descent to Lochan na Ciste.

CREAG COIRE NA CISTE

This buttress is contained by Number Three and Four Gullies. It comprises a series of minor buttresses and gullies of considerable steepness.

120   **South Gully**   125m   III

G. G. Macphee   April 1936

Start from the foot of the narrow section of Number Three Gully, level with the lowest rocks of Number Three Gully Buttress.

Climb an obvious ledge slanting right to the foot of a steep gully which slants back up to the left. Under heavy snow it can be a straightforward climb, but normally provides two pitches and sometimes a large cornice. *Diagram page 96-97.*

121   Central Gully   125m   III

I. S. Clough and J. M. Alexander   January 1959

This follows a line just left of the Central Rib.

Start at the lowest rocks and climb by a series of snow patches left of the rib to the foot of two parallel ice gullies (70m). Climb the left gully on steep ice (35m). Cross into the righthand gully and climb on snow to the plateau. *Diagram page 96-97.*

The righthand gully can be climbed throughout and is harder.

122   Central Rib   125m   Difficult

M. W. Erlebach and E. C. Pyatt   July 1941

Start at the lowest point of the crag; climb by a rock rib in a series of short pitches to where the rib steepens and becomes well defined (70m). Continue by the left edge overlooking a narrow chimney-gully (50m). This section ends on a ledge which leads easily left under the final tower to the plateau. *Diagram page 96-97.*

The tower may be climbed by rightward slanting grooves to the left of the two obvious cracks (Very Difficult).

WINTER   III

R. N.Campbell and J. R. Marshall   March 1970

Climb the route as for summer. If the steep pitch on the upper rocks proves insurmountable, it can be turned by a brief move into the gully on the left, as on the first winter ascent.

123   North Gully   110m   II

J. Y. MacDonald and H. W. Turnbull   March 1934

Start half-way between the lowest rocks of Creag Coire na Ciste on the left and the narrows of Number Four Gully on the right, at the foot of a narrow gully.

The foot of the gully is masked by steep snow which leads to the gully narrows. Normally there is a steep 12m ice pitch. The route then leads over easier snow and ice to the cornice which is rarely difficult. *Diagram page 96-97.*

VARIATION—LEFT FORK   35m   III

D. Bathgate, J. Knight and A. McKeith   February 1964

From the snow basin near the top of North Gully, climb up left into a steepening snow scoop, then up a steep iced groove at its back to the cornice and the top.

124   NUMBER FOUR GULLY

This gully separates Creag Coire na Ciste from the rock mass of the Trident Buttresses. Above the great scree slopes beyond the Lochan na Ciste, Number Four Gully trends to the right, partially hidden behind the South Trident Buttress and gains the plateau at the lowest point between Ben Nevis and Carn Dearg. It is marked at its top by a marker post to aid in identification in poor conditions. It is an important winter descent from the plateau.

In summer it provides an easy scramble over loose scree with no pitches. *Diagram page 41, 96-97 and 107.*

WINTER   100m   I

W. W. Naismith, A. E. Maylard and F. C. Squance   Easter 1895

The gully provides an easy snow climb and probably the easiest descent from the plateau.

SOUTH TRIDENT BUTTRESS

This is the most southerly and best defined of the Trident Buttresses. It is sharply defined on the right or north by the gully of the Central Trident and on the left by Number Four Gully and its attendant screes.

The buttress comprises three tiers. The lowest is steep, with the routes on it leading to the upper reaches of a broad grassy ledge. This point can easily be gained from the screes under Number Four Gully. The middle tier commences above the ledge and is defined above by a similar but smaller ledge raking up from the narrows of Number Four Gully. The final tier is a narrow, shattered ridge which provides scrambling to the summit screes.

H

125   1944 Route   125m   Severe

B. P. Kellett   July 1944

This is a superb climb.

Scramble to the foot of the steep wall 30m right of the lowest rocks.

Climb left to a steep chimney, then trend left to a ledge and belay (24m). Climb from a large, leaning block to the foot of the second groove from the left; traverse right under the third groove to a point beneath the fourth and rightmost groove (24m). Climb into the groove, then, using a crack in the right wall, reach a system of ledges which are followed to a steep corner (34m). Finish by the corner in 12m to gain the middle ledge near its northern end. *Diagram page 107.*

The next five routes ascend the middle tier of the buttress and can be approached either by lower routes, or by traversing the terrace from the screes of Number Four Gully.

126   Strident Edge   100m   Very Severe

N. Muir and D. Regan   July 1972

The route follows the obvious sharp arete between Spartacus and Sidewinder (see below) and is easier than its appearance would suggest.

Start 6m left of the chimney of Sidewinder and climb to belays on that route (15m). Move out right and climb the steep crack to belay on the crest (36m). Follow the outer left edge to the top of the middle tier. *Diagram page 107.*

127   Sidewinder   99m   Very Severe

J. R. Marshall, R. Marshall and A. Wightman   June 1964

The route is on the south face of the middle tier of the buttress. Look for a triple-tiered corner rising steeply leftwards across the face and starting 15m to the right of an obvious flake chimney (The Groove Climb. Very Difficult).

Scramble from the ledge to the foot of the corner (23m). Climb the corner by cracks in three pitches of 15m, 10m and 21m to gain an easy slab. Continue directly by the line of the crack and a large flake to gain the crest of the buttress below the final tier (30m). Not shown on diagram.

13 Strident Edge, pitch two (Ken Crocket).   *Photo: C. Stead*

128   **Spartacus**   97m   Very Severe
I. S. Clough and G. Grandison   June 1962

Start from the ledge under the rocks of the middle tier and traverse beneath the arete of Strident Edge to the foot of a corner. This is 20m left of the great corner, a major feature of this tier of the buttress.

Climb the corner, surmount the overhang, then traverse right to a stance and peg belay (28m). Follow a little groove on the right to a flake, descend a little, cross the steep wall to an arete, then climb to a large flake belay (15m). Continue directly, then left above the overhang to a flake crack. Follow this a short way, then traverse right to belays on an arete (24m). Climb the groove above to the top of the middle tier (30m). *Diagram page 107.*

129   **The Slab Climb**   91m   Very Difficult
B. P. Kellett   July 1944

This climb offers good rock and situations.

Start midway between Spartacus and the great corner.

Climb the righthand of two cracks to an overhang, traverse into the left crack to stance and belay (24m). Continue by the crack to a conspicuous chimney (24m). Climb the strenuous chimney (15m). It can be avoided on the left. Follow the chimney to the top of the tier (28m). *Diagram page 107.*

130   **Pinnacle Arete**   150m   Very Difficult
H. Raeburn and Dr and Mrs Inglis Clark   June 1902

Start from the rightmost end of the middle ledge at a point overlooking the steep north wall of the buttress.

Climb sloping ledges for 3m, then an awkward corner on the right, followed by 10m of difficult rock to easier ground. Trend left onto the crest and climb to the foot of a steep wall; climb this direct on good holds. A further short, steep section leads to the narrow, shattered crest and the final tier of the buttress which gives scrambling to the summit plateau. *Diagram page 107.*

WINTER   **IV**
R. H. Sellars and J. Smith   February 1959

Follow a snow traverse across the middle ledge then, by a series of snow and ice grooves immediately right of the crest, reach the easier upper section of the buttress.

14
South and Central Trident Buttresses of Ben Nevis

ST	*South Trident Buttress*	**130**	*Pinnacle Arete*
CT	*Central Trident Buttress*	**131**	*Central Gully*
124	*Number Four Gully*	**132**	*Jubilee Climb*
125	*1944 Route*	**133**	*Jubilation*
126	*Strident Edge*	**134**	*Steam*
128	*Spartacus*	**135**	*Heidbanger*
129	*The Slab Climb*	**136**	*Metamorphosis*

131 **Central Gully**   240m   III

H. Raeburn, Mrs W. and Mr C. Inglis Clark   April 1904

This gully defines the right or northern flank of the South Trident Buttress and lies almost directly above Lochan na Ciste.

The gully fills up well and normally snow, interrupted by one short ice pitch, leads to the steep ice column well seen from below. The original party turned this on the left by mixed snow and ice to regain the upper snow bay at the earliest opportunity. The steep upper buttress was turned on the left by a gully, then regained above the steep section and followed to the top. *Diagram page 107.*

The steep ice column may be climbed direct (III).

CENTRAL TRIDENT BUTTRESS

This is the indeterminate area of rock to the right of Central Gully which extends northwards to merge with the rocks of the North Trident Buttress. There are some fine rock climbs on the steep central section.

132 **Jubilee Climb**   240m   Very Difficult

G. G. Macphee, G. C. Williams and D. Henderson   May 1935

From the bifurcation in the lower reaches of Central Gully, take the shallow righthand branch over easy slabs and scree for 75m until below a corner and crack. Climb this for 3m, traverse right over blocks to belay. Climb the slabs above for 12m, then scree for 12m to a short chimney and slab which lead in 30m to a scree slope.

The upper buttress can be seen higher on the left, gain the base and climb by the crest in two steep pitches (75m). Scrambling leads to the final slopes of Carn Dearg. *Diagram page 107.*

WINTER   II

D. Haston and R. Smith   1961

The route gives an interesting climb on snow with some small ice pitches leading to the middle terrace, whence a choice of lines lead to the top. Care should be taken in avalanche conditions.

133   Jubilation   240m   III
R. Marshall, J. R. Marshall and J. Stenhouse   December 1963

Climb the Jubilee Route to the 3m pitch. Traverse left into twin chimneys and climb the rightmost chimney on steep ice to a snow bay (18m). Regain the left branch and climb 24m on ice to easier chimneys which are followed to the final arete of the buttress. *Diagram page 107.*

The following three routes ascend the impressive, steep rock wall which lies below and to the right of the Jubilee Climb.

134   Steam   100m   Extremely Severe E1
S. Docherty and B. Gorman   Summer 1970

Start at an obvious corner groove 24m left of the prominent, large crack system splitting the face.

Climb to an overhang which is turned on the left to a stance and peg belay (24m). Climb the wall above for 6m, then move left to a corner. Climb this to a leftward sloping ramp and belay in a greasy corner (30m). Traverse diagonally up and right and mantelshelf left on to a sloping ledge (peg runner). Continue left and climb a steep wall to the top of the buttress (36m). The upper rocks of the Jubilee Climb can now be followed to the summit plateau, or the lower section of that route descended. *Diagram page 107.*

135   Heidbanger   90m   Extremely Severe E1
N. Muir and I. Nicholson   June 1970

A very good climb.

Start 6m left of the base of the prominent crack system which splits the face.

Climb a bulge and move right to the top of a steep groove on the right at 6m, then climb a short corner onto the band of slabs. Traverse rightwards to the arete and belay in the cave of the crack system (36m). Climb the crack and follow a line of weakness up the wall leftwards to belay on the arete (24m). Take a line from the corner on the left, by walls and corners to the top (30m). *Diagram page 107.*

VARIATION   21m   Extremely Severe E1
N. Muir and A. Paul   June 1977

This, a direct start is the more proper route and climbs the large crack to the cave at 21m to rejoin the original route.

136 **Metamorphosis**   105m   Extremely Severe E1
S. Docherty and D. Gardner   *August 1971*

Another fine climb to complete a hard trilogy.

Start just left of an overhanging crack at the right end of the face some 25m right of Heidbanger.

Climb right to join the crack below the bulge, surmount this and continue to below a corner. Go right and up to the corner (peg runner) and follow it to a ledge and peg belay (36m). Continue past a recess to a ledge, traverse right, then up to a peg belay and poor stance beneath a prominent flake (27m). Climb the flake and wall above, then trend right to easier ground (27m). Finish by a corner and wall above (15m). *Diagram page 107.*

NORTH TRIDENT BUTTRESS

The rocks of this buttress form the northern, or right edge of the main mass of the Trident Buttresses.

Easy angled rocks at the base lead to twin ridges separated by a gully. These ridges can also be reached by the steep rock face further along the base of the buttress.

137 **Neptune Gully**   160m   III
A. J. Bennet and J. Clarkson   *February 1956*

This is the gully which splits the northern, or righthand crest of the buttress and lies to the left of the Original Route (see below).

Climb the snow-covered rocks of the Original Route to an ice pitch barring access to the gully. Climb this on the right, then continue up the gully over three short pitches to snow slopes leading to a large platform overlooking Number Five Gully. Climb by the easy ridge and slopes above to the plateau. *Diagram page 111.*

138 **Original Route**   160m   Very Difficult

The route ascends the indefinite rocks on the right edge of the buttress, defined on the right by Moonlight Gully.

Start by the rocks of a trap dyke and climb without difficulty to a broad ledge (45m). Trend left to climb the righthand ridge leading to the foot of the final tower (75m). Climb the steep, exposed edge (21m). Beyond the scree above, the final rocks provide moderate climbing. *Diagram page 111.*

North Trident and Moonlight Gully Buttresses of Ben Nevis

15

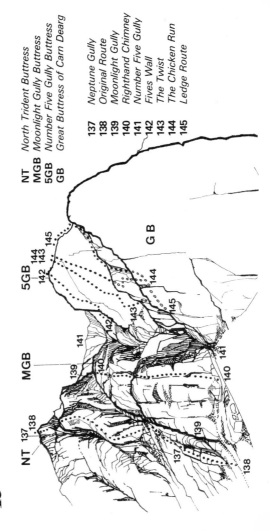

NT	*North Trident Buttress*
MGB	*Moonlight Gully Buttress*
5GB	*Number Five Gully Buttress*
GB	*Great Buttress of Carn Dearg*

137	*Neptune Gully*
138	*Original Route*
139	*Moonlight Gully*
140	*Righthand Chimney*
141	*Number Five Gully*
142	*Fives Wall*
143	*The Twist*
144	*The Chicken Run*
145	*Ledge Route*

WINTER   IV

J. Maclay, H. Raeburn, C. W. Walker and H. Walker   January 1904

The lower rocks are generally masked in snow, thereafter the difficulties are fairly continuous with mixed climbing to the final tower. This can be climbed direct, but is extremely difficult, otherwise the tower can be turned and the upper section of the buttress followed to the top.

139 **Moonlight Gully**   150m   I

W. Inglis Clark and T. Gibson   January 1908

This is the straight, narrow gully which runs between North Trident Buttress on the left and Moonlight Gully Buttress on the right.

It gives a straightforward snow ascent which debouches into the upper funnel of Number Five Gully. *Diagram page 111.*

MOONLIGHT GULLY BUTTRESS

This is the two-tiered section of rock which lies between Moonlight Gully and the lower reaches of Number Five Gully.

140 **Righthand Chimney**   120m   Very Difficult

G. Scott, E. M. Hanlon and B. P. Kellett   July 1943

Start midway between the gullies at the foot of the rightmost and better defined of the chimneys splitting the buttress. Follow the chimney throughout, steep and sustained for 60m. Thereafter easier climbing leads to the top of the first tier. Climb with little difficulty by the continuation of the chimney on the upper tier (30m). *Diagram page 111.*

141 **Number Five Gully**   460m   Easy

The gully separates the Trident Buttresses from the Great Buttress of Carn Dearg. It is a wide, shallow gully opening out to become virtually a coire in its upper reaches.

A rib of rock divides the gully, the left branch is drier and easier; higher up a large chockstone is passed by a through route. If this is too wet, a rib on the left can be climbed. In the upper section, the true gully trends up to the right between rock ribs leading almost to the summit of Carn Dearg. *Diagram page 41, 111 and 126, 127.*

WINTER   I

N. J. Collie and party   Easter 1895

The summer pitches can present short ice steps, otherwise the climb is on snow. Cornices can be massive above the gully, but the rim is extensive and an easy exit should always be available.

Care should be exercised in avalanche conditions.

NUMBER FIVE GULLY BUTTRESS

This is the steep exposure of rock which stands halfway up the right flank of Number Five Gully.

Above the lower narrows of the gully, a broad scree ledge leads out rightwards into a bay under the north wall of the buttress and a short expanse of rock which extends to the north.

142 **Fives Wall** 60m Severe

J. R. Marshall and C. L. Donaldson   September 1953

Halfway up the Number Five Gully face of the buttress is a curving grass ledge, follow this to the far end to a cairn marking the start of the route.

Climb a groove to a ledge, traverse right beyond its end, then up to a large flake. Climb this, then cracks to reach a large slab ledge. Traverse left, climb a short crack and wall to a large ledge. Further right a steep crack leads to the buttress top. *Diagram page 111.*

143 **The Twist** 150m Very Severe

I. S. Clough and G. Grandison   June 1962

This is a good, but devious route.

Start at the lowest point of the buttress, under a steep corner.

Climb a short, steep groove to a ledge at the foot of a gangway and continue to a peg belay under a little corner crack (12m). Climb the crack, then up to a spike belay (12m). Continue to the top of the gangway, move right, then left to belay below a cracked slab (15m). Traverse right to gain sloping ledges above the overhanging wall, belays (12m). Climb diagonally right over a big flake, then horizontally by sloping shelves to a peg belay under a corner (18m). Climb the corner (15m). Traverse right, then up to a chockstone belay by a pinnacle

(20m). Follow the cracks above to the top of a huge pedestal block, chockstone belay (15m). Gain the ledge above, climb into a groove on the left, then out right to a large block; finish up left to reach a grass ledge (22m). Scramble to the top. *Diagram page 111.*

144   The Chicken Run   150m   Very Severe
J. R. Marshall and J. Stenhouse   May 1961

The route offers fine situations.

Start 45m up to the right from the lowest rocks of the buttress.

Climb a steep crack to a ledge (27m). Continue slightly right on shattered rock to rock ledge (12m). Traverse this left to gain a great flake (15m). Climb the wall above to a ledge (12m). Follow a series of cracks and awkward corners to a larger ledge. Finish more easily. *Diagram page 111.*

145   Ledge Route   450m   Easy
J. S. Napier, R. G. Napier and E. W. Green   June 1895

An enjoyable outing through interesting scenery.

Start up Number Five Gully, break out right on to the third ledge from the foot of the gully and follow this until it becomes impracticable. A shallow gully then leads up left to a higher ledge which is again followed to the right. This eventually leads to the easy angled crest of the Great Buttress and to a platform on which a large cairn has been erected. Follow the crest above to the summit plateau. *Diagram page 111.*

WINTER   II
S.M.C. Party   Easter 1897

Under normal conditions the route gives an interesting ascent on snow.

THE GREAT BUTTRESS OF CARN DEARG

This lies to the right of Number Five Gully. When viewed from the C.I.C. Hut, the buttress presents a magnificent face of overlapping slabs and great overhangs, probably unmatched anywhere in the country. The righthand, or northern flank of the buttress turns, in an impressively steep wall to a junction with Waterfall Gully. The buttress is cut by the huge corner line of Centurion to the left and the corner-chimney line of Sassenach to the right.

146   The Curtain   110m   IV
J. Knight and D. Bathgate   February 1965

This route follows the huge cataract of ice which forms on the buttress edge, just right of Number Five Gully. It gives a good introduction to steep ice climbing.

Start in a large slab corner and climb ice to belay below the upper wall. Climb this in two pitches by the line of least resistance to a junction with the easy slopes of Ledge Route. *Diagram page 126-127.*

147   Route I   215m   Very Difficult
A. T. Hargreaves, G. G. Macphee and H. V. Hughes   June 1931

This is a classic of its grade.

Start to the left of the lowest rocks of the minor, curving buttress which lies on the lower, left flank of the buttress.

Climb to a ledge and belay (13m), then by the right edge to a big ledge (18m). Scramble by grassy cracks left to a big block belay (10m). Continue left, then follow the grooves above to easier climbing leading to the top of the minor buttress.

Walk right to the foot of an obvious chimney and climb this, finishing by a grassy groove to a recess and belay (21m). Climb the right wall for 6m to a belay. Regain the chimney 3m higher and climb to a stance and spike belay (15m). Move out left and climb an exposed slab to belay at the foot of the final chimney (8m). Climb the chimney to a broad ledge at 12m. Walk right and climb easier rocks to gain the Ledge Route. *Diagram page 126-127.*

WINTER   IV
D. Knowles and D. Wilson   Winter 1972

Not often in winter condition.

Climb the lower section as for summer, or avoid the minor buttress by traversing in from the left to the foot of the chimney. Climb this with progressive difficulty to the top.

14 The Curtain, pitch one (Stuart Smith). *Photo: K. V. Crocket*

148 **Route II** 150m Severe

B. P. Kellett and W. A. Russell June 1943

This is a superb route with tremendous situations.

Climb Route I to the foot of the chimney section above the minor buttress. Climb the chimney for 12m, traverse the slab on the right for 6m to a small stance and good belay. Trend up right in two pitches of 10m and 15m to reach a large flake beneath the great overhangs. Climb above the flake, traverse right on lush vegetation to a platform with an inconspicuous thread belay low down (12m). This section is better climbed by traversing the flake for 6m then ascending the rock rib to the thread belay. Traverse across the buttress to the right in two pitches of 30m and 10m to gain a platform on the edge of the buttress. Scramble up the edge for 30m, then enter a groove which is followed, mainly on the right wall for two pitches of 21m and 12m to gain the buttress crest. *Diagram page 126-127.*

VARIATION—DIRECT START 75m Severe

B. W. Robertson and G. Chisholm May 1962

A worthwhile variant to give a more sustained route.

Start at a cairn on a grass ledge right of the lowest rocks of Route I. Climb the centre of a smooth slab to a small ledge, traverse a little right to a wall, then by a small, slanting corner to traverse left to a stance. Finish by a small black crack to a flake belay (30m). Climb straight up to a large block below a groove (15m). Climb the groove, then traverse round an arete on the right to a shattered ledge (10m). Continue by the bulge above to easier ground and a small belay near the chimney of Route I (24m). *Diagram page 126-127.*

WINTER V

M. Geddes and A. Rouse February 1978

The first winter ascent approximately followed the summer line, but the ascent of Route II Direct only a few days later produced a much better climb.

ROUTE II DIRECT V

G. Smith and I. Sykes February 1978

A magnificent route, rarely in genuine winter condition. It requires a good plating of snow and ice.

Start in a deep corner at the lowest point of rock right of Route I.

Climb the corner for 24m, then traverse left under a roof on to Route II Direct Start, which is followed to the large ledge below the chimney of Route I. Continue above by the summer line of Route II. The lower section is much harder than the upper.

149   **The Shadow**   245m   Very Severe

T. Sullivan and N. Collingham   September 1959

This pleasant climb is low in its grade.

Start a few metres right of Route I at the foot of a long, thin crack.

Climb the crack, then traverse right to a belay (27m). Surmount the block above, round a corner, then follow a little groove to a grass ledge (12m). Climb the wall above and step right to enter a grassy groove (27m). Follow the groove until it widens, then traverse 10m right to block belays (36m). Climb up, then traverse left below a black slab to break through the overlap; continue to a small corner (40m). Make an ascending right traverse across a wet streak to the grassy groove of Centurion (40m). Climb up right to belay in a grassy corner on the crest of the buttress (36m). Climb the right wall of the corner and traverse left across another slab to a ledge (24m). Finish by the groove above (24m). *Diagram page 126-127.*

WINTER   V

P. Braithwaite and D. Pearce   March 1979

The summer route is followed and gives a very hard climb.

150   **The Bullroar**   245m   Hard Very Severe

J. R. Marshall and J. Stenhouse   May 1961

A superb climb taking a rising traverse across the face of the buttress.

Start 30m right of Route I at some large boulders.

Climb up into a groove and on to a flake belay (27m). Move up left into a parallel groove which is followed to a belay (15m). This belay may be gained directly. Traverse the slabs right, under the overlap to reach a crack which is climbed to a belay (13m). Descend and continue the traverse to a stance and peg belay (15m). Continue the traverse, ascending to gain the belay above pitch three of Centurion (30m). Climb the crack above, then traverse right to a stance and peg belay (27m). Move right then up to reach the terrace above the chimneys of the Bat and Sassenach (30m). From the left end of the terrace, traverse to an area of shattered rocks beneath an undercut groove (12m). Climb the groove and continue above by a series of corners and slabby grooves to the top of the buttress. *Diagram page 126-127.*

151 **Adrenalin Rush** 235m Extremely Severe E3

K. Johnstone and W. Todd Summer 1978

Start at a large boulder 10m right of Bullroar.

Climb the crack on the left side of the boulder, then by the groove above to step left to a ledge (15m). Move up and left to the right side of a large, detached block. Step up, then right to gain a groove directly above, belay. Climb groove to a roof, step right to underclings, then directly over the roof to a slab. Move diagonally right for 8m, then back left along the lip of the next overlap to belay below a corner (36m). Follow the corner line over an overhang at 12m. Continue up crackline to belay in large corner 9m below a big roof (40m). Move on to a rib on the left, climb up until possible to traverse right along the lip of the roof. Pull on to a hanging slab and cross this to a belay on its right edge (33m). Step down and traverse right 10m to the foot of a shallow groove. Climb this for 6m, step left, then move up a corner and across a slab on the right to belay below a wide, diagonal crack (junction with Centurion, 26m). Cross a slab on the left to a corner. Cross the left wall of the corner to a slab rib, then up the slab to finish by an undercut groove on the left (37m). *Diagram page 126-127.*

152 **Cowslip** 140m Extremely Severe E2

R. Carrington and I. Nicholson April 1970

The route follows the line of the "weep", i.e. the great dark streak which emanates from the garden patch on Route II. It is rarely wholly dry.

Start just left of Torro (see below) and follow a smooth groove up left to a small stance below a bank of overhangs. Climb up into a steep groove, gain a slab on the left (awkward), then by a delicate left traverse, reach an overlap which is followed right to its lowest point. Climb on to the small slab above and move up to climb the black, overhanging corner above (poor protection). Continue more easily by the slabs above to reach the traverse ledge of Route II. Finish by one of the routes which breach the upper overhangs of the buttress. *Diagram page 126-127.*

153 Torro 215m Extremely Severe E1

J. McLean, W. Smith and W. Gordon   July 1962

This very fine climb starts just left of the foot of the rib which forms the left wall of the great corner of Centurion, about 30m right of The Bullroar.

Climb an overhanging groove to a flake runner. Climb the groove above to a large flake, ascend the righthand side, move back left and continue up a groove to a good stance and large flake belay (30m). Climb a widening fault, then a bulge on the left to the edge of the slab (peg runner). Traverse left across the slab, step round the corner, then go up an overhanging groove to a good stance and flake belay (24m). Climb diagonally right round a bulge to enter a crack, climb this for 6m, move slightly right, then up slab to good stance and peg belay (24m). Climb a slight crack 8m and step left onto a higher slab. Move across the slab 3m and climb the overhang above trending left, finishing by the groove above in 6m to a good stance and peg belay (21m). Climb a fault for 5m, traverse the slab right to a crack, follow this to an overhang which is climbed trending left, then finish by a groove to reach a grassy stance and peg belay (42m). Continue up a fault to a grass ledge beneath large overhangs, peg belay (30m). Climb up to the overhang, move left on to a steep slab. Go up left to another overhang and step from a detached flake to traverse delicately up left on to a large slab. Continue up right for 12m to a stance and peg belay (33m). Traverse left to a large corner, climb into this and continue to a grass terrace. *Diagram page 126-127.*

154 Centurion 215m Hard Very Severe

D. D. Whillans and R. O. Downes   August 1956

This is one of the great classics of Ben Nevis. It takes the huge corner-groove which is such a prominent feature of the lower part of the buttress.

Start at the undercut base of the groove and climb the left wall to a large platform, move right to enter the groove and climb to a ledge and belays (15m). Continue by the corner, which affords good protection, to a slab stance in an overhung bay (36m). Traverse left on to the edge, follow easy grooves, step right on to the lip of a big overhang, then climb up to a stance and peg belay (24m). Move back into the corner, traverse left up the wall below the overhanging crack, then follow the arete to a stance (21m). Climb slabby grooves by the same line to a small stance and block belay (21m). Continue in the same line, then move left to the stance before the long traverse of Route II (18m). Climb up to the

15 Adrenalin Rush, first ascent (Willie Todd). *Photo: K. Johnstone*

16 Torro, pitch one.

Photo: C. Stead

overhang and move left to a steep slab. Go left up to another overhang, then step from a detached flake to traverse delicately up left on to a large slab. Climb this easily up to the right to stance and belay below the second tier of overhangs (27m). Traverse right for 6m, then climb a spiky arete to a bulge, above which step left into an easy groove leading to a broad ledge (24m). *Diagram page 126-127.*

WINTER   V
R. Millward   1975

On the only winter ascent recorded to date, the first three pitches were climbed over verglased rock, abseiled off, then continued next day to the traverse of Route II, which was then followed.

155 **King Kong**   300m   Extremely Severe E1
B. W. Robertson, F. Harper and J. Graham   September 1964

The route follows a complex line up the right edge of the fine slabs on the right wall of the Centurion corner, aiming for the vertical crack high on the right. The route finding is difficult and inadvertent, hard variations have been made. The original route used many points of aid, but these have since been eliminated.

Climb the first pitch of Centurion. Traverse out right on the slabs for 6m and rope down 3m to a lower slab, then traverse right to an open corner, aid used (21m). Climb the corner (peg) to gain a sloping slab, then up to a corner and junction with The Bat. Make a descending left traverse past the block belay to the big, loose block, peg belay (33m). These diversions seem pointless and the route is more commonly started from the second pitch of The Bat (see below).

Climb up left over a slab to the first overlap, surmount this, then traverse right to climb a chockstone crack on the second overlap. From the slab above, descend right, then up to a small ledge under a smooth groove. Move left, then right to below a bulge. Swing right to a scoop and peg belay (27m). Take a line left, then up to a huge overhang, climb a 2.5m overlap to the right, then traverse right to a sloping ledge below a vertical crack which is climbed to a small ledge and peg belay (18m). Continue by the crack, then traverse easily right to climb an arete. Continue slightly left to a smooth slab and belay just left of the belay at the top of the Bat corner (27m). Traverse left over a slab, climb a wide crack to a small overlap, climb this and the crack in the upper slab to climb a large overlap direct. Climb the slab above going slightly right to another large overlap. Climb this by a crack, then by slabs and an easy, broken overlap, climb up left to a small grass ledge and peg belay (40m). Climb easily by a grassy bay to a vertical wall, traverse left and up to a block belay below an overhanging wall capped by a small roof (18m). Climb the wall by a crack, cross the overhang, then move left and up a slab corner, making for a huge roof, to take a peg belay under an overhanging corner (40m). Climb the corner, swing across to a spike, move left, then up to a stance and spike (40m). Continue slightly right, then up to a grassy groove. Move left, then up to finish (30m). *Diagram page 126-127.*

156   The Bat   303m   Extremely Severe E1

D. Haston and R. Smith   September 1959

A modern classic.

Climb the first pitch of Centurion (15m). Enter the corner, at 10m traverse out right by slabs to a large block then, by the shelf, continue right to a block belay (33m). Descend 3m, then move up and right by a shelf, into a corner, over a short wall to a triangular slab. Follow the V-groove above, then by slabs trend right to belay under the Sassenach chimney (27m). Turn the edge on the left, then climb a short groove to gain the corner above (12m). Climb the corner direct (30m). Follow the groove to the left end of a terrace (33m). Move right and climb into an undercut groove just above the Sassenach chimney (33m). Continue by the line of the grooves above, belays as required (120m). *Diagram page 126-127.*

157   Sassenach   290m   Hard Very Severe

J. Brown and D. D. Whillans   April 1954

This is a magnificent, old-fashioned classic, somewhat neglected nowadays.

Start below and to the right of the great chimney corner where a large slab of rock leans against the face.

From just left of the slab, climb sloping, mossy ledges for 6m until it is possible to step right onto a nose. Traverse left to the foot of a crack and climb this to a stance and belay (33m). Climb the corner above (2 slings for aid if wet) and traverse left and up below the overhang to belays at the foot of the huge chimney (27m). Climb the chimney in two pitches to a grassy terrace (52m). Move up and right by the terrace to the foot of a V-groove capped by an overhang (18m). Climb the groove for

10m, step out left to a ledge. Continue by the crack above to enter another groove (33m). Climb the groove to step right at the top (12m). Enter the grooves above which continue in 95m to the top of the buttress. *Diagram page 126-127.*

158   Caligula   114m   Extremely Severe E3
D. Cuthbertson, D. Mullin and W. Todd   June 1978

The climb follows the very steep line between Sassenach and Titan's Wall (previously known as the Big Banana Groove).

Climb the first pitch of Titan's Wall (see below). Traverse left round the arete and continue to a small ledge and belay at the foot of the groove (12m). Climb the corner and step left to a foot ledge and hanging belay on the arete (18m). Climb the rib above for a few moves, then traverse right into the groove. Follow the groove a short way, then traverse right to a small ledge and belay (15m). Step up and left to gain a thin, diagonal crack; climb this and an overhang, then continue along a right trending ramp to a crack. Climb the crack and continue to a stance and belay at the top of Titan's Wall (33m). *Diagram page 126-127.*

159   Titan's Wall   115m   Extremely Severe E4
I. S. Clough and H. MacInnes   April 1959

This route follows a line of cracks on the vertical north wall of the buttress. Originally climbed with aid, its free ascent now provides one of the finest and hardest routes on the mountain.

Start 12m along the foot of the north wall and climb by cracks to an overhang at 15m, which is climbed to follow the crack line trending right to a ledge. Traverse this left until above the overhang, peg belay (36m). Return along the ledge, rejoin the crack line and continue over bulges to a ledge and belay (45m). Climb up to the left, then right, to enter a groove which is followed to a junction with the upper pitches of Sassenach (30m). Finish by that route to the top of the buttress. *Diagram page 142-143.*

160   The Shield   110m   Hard Very Severe
D. D. Whillans and R. O. Downes   September 1956

This route gives good chimney climbing.

The north wall of the buttress is defined on the right by Waterfall Gully. Above the huge introductory pitch of this gully, an enormous

16
The Great Buttress
of
Carn Dearg

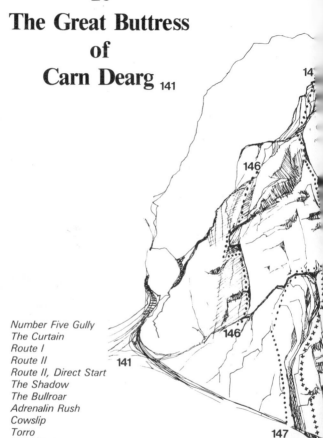

flake stands against the north wall, forming a chimney. This is the line of the route.

Climb as for Evening Wall (see below) to gain Waterfall Gully (24m). Cross the gully, scramble to a broad glacis, then descend grass to the foot of the chimney (45m). Climb the chimney, awkward to a small grass ledge (18m). Follow the chimney until it is possible to step left to a small cave, thread belay (12m). Regain the chimney, surmount a difficult bulge and continue to a belay (40m). Continue by the chimney, becoming grassy, to gain the top of the flake (36m). The route now joins Evening Wall which is followed to the buttress top. *Diagram page 142-143.*

VARIATION—DIRECT START   70m   Hard Very Severe

J. R. Marshall, R. Marshall and G. J. Ritchie   June 1962

Good climbing.

Start at the foot of the north wall of the buttress, 6m right of Titan's Wall and just left of the deep cracks of the corner.

Climb the wall for 5m, traverse right into the crack and climb to belays (24m). Follow the crack until under the great roof; move on to the left wall then, with aid, climb a thin crack to surmount the left edge of the roof. From the stance above, climb a short chimney to stance and belay (15m). Continue by the line of the chimney to a block belay (18m). Climb the steep groove above and traverse right to join The Shield above the first chimney pitch (18m). *Diagram page 142-143.*

WINTER   VI

M. Fowler and A. Saunders   March 1979

This very hard climb starts in the corner just right of that followed by Shield Direct.

Climb in two pitches to gain the foot of the chimney of The Shield which is then followed to the upper section of the buttress where a choice of lines lead to the top.

161 **Evening Wall**   245m   Very Difficult

C. F. Rolland and H. I. Ogilvy   June 1940

A fine climb.

Climb a clean-cut chimney 10m right of the foot of Waterfall Gully. Exit by the left wall and climb to a block belay (24m). Continue above for 6m, cross the gully on the left and climb the far wall by a difficult edge, followed by slabs to gain grass (30m). Climb an easy angled chimney for 15m, then a rightward trending groove on the wall above, to reach raking slabs leading up to the base of an enormous flake (36m). Climb a chimney to the top of the flake (10m). Traverse left over grass and easy rock to a flake belay (30m). Gain the crest of the buttress and climb up left, then make a short traverse right and up to gain a large ledge (21m). Move left along the ledge, descend slightly to reach the foot of twin grooves, climb the right one for 10m to a belay. Continue by the groove to the top of the buttress (60m). *Diagram page 142-143.*

162   Gemini   300m   V

A. Paul and D. Sanderson   March 1979

Climb Waterfall Gully for 69m to the rightward trending groove of Evening Wall. Follow this to the enormous flake of that route. Climb the ice wall directly above to rightward sloping grooves. Follow these for 60m to obvious twin grooves of Evening Wall. Follow either groove to a broad ledge. Traverse the ledge right for 15m and climb iced slabs leading in 45m to easy ground. *Diagram page 142-143.*

163   Waterfall Gully   215m   IV

D. Pipes, I. S. Clough, J. M. Alexander, R. Shaw and A. Flegg   January 1959

The gully defines the north flank of the Great Buttress of Carn Dearg, rising initially in one great step 30m high, thereafter easily to gain the saddle behind the pinnacle of the Staircase Climb. It gives a mediocre climb.

Start 20m right of Titan's Wall, up a steep ice pitch for 25m, then more easily to the upper gully. A further short ice pitch, then snow leads easily to the gully exit.

The slabby rocks in the exit area may present a hazard in avalanche conditions. *Diagram page 142-143.*

164   Staircase Climb   215m   Very Difficult

J. H. Bell, J. Maclay and W. W. Naismith   July 1898

Start up to the right of Evening Wall by the higher of two shelves sloping up right round a corner.

Once round the corner, follow the stepped slab right to the foot of a clean-cut crack in a corner (15m). Climb the crack, then the short wall above to a platform (8m). Continue by a chimney above to easy ground

(15m). Scramble by the crest of the buttress making for a conspicuous pinnacle (60m). Turn the pinnacle on the left, descending into Waterfall Gully, then up, to climb a steep slab to the saddle behind the pinnacle. Climb the left hand of two chimneys above for 45m to reach easier climbing following a ridge up left to the summit rocks of the Great Buttress of Carn Dearg. *Diagram page 142-143.*

WINTER   IV

D. Haston and J. Stenhouse   February 1957

The buttress gives a good mixed ascent followed as for summer. Under light cover, the "clean-cut crack" and the pinnacle section can be quite awkward.

NORTH WALL OF CARN DEARG

This is the name given to the northern flank of the Carn Dearg Great Buttress. Although traversed by several large ledges, the intervening walls are impressively steep and provide fine climbing.

165   Zag-Zig   55m   Severe

I. S. Clough, R. Porteous, P. Brocklehurst and R. Henson   May 1959

Start about 30m from the left edge and follow the zigzag fault up the steep wall below the obvious, broad grass rake.

Climb up to the grassy lower crack and traverse it to a stance and belay (27m). Move right up the chimney by a stomach traverse; half-way one is forced onto the wall. The finish is an awkward exit from a cave, well protected by chockstone runners. *Diagram page 142-143.*

166   Kellett's North Wall Route   178m   Severe

B. P. Kellett, J. H. B. Bell, N. Forsyth and C. M. Plackett   1943

This route was originally climbed in separate sorties by Kellett, solo or in the company of members of the party as noted.

It is a tremendous climb, but inclined to be greasy.

Start to the right of the broad grass rake 50m from the left edge of the face, at a large flake with a deep chimney to the right.

Climb the chimney to exit by a window in the flake (24m). Scramble to a broad ledge (6m). Continue above to the foot of a conspicuous crack (3m). Climb the strenuous crack to gain the crest of a flake terrace (18m). About 6m to the right from the secondary point of the flake, gain a groove in the steep wall and climb to a large grass recess (8m). Make an exposed traverse right on to a rib, then climb directly by a crack to easier rocks (12m). Continue by the crack to an upper terrace and block belay (8m). Traverse right to an open corner (15m). Climb to the right of the corner to a ledge and thread belay beneath a steep, exposed slab with two thin cracks, belay (6m). Climb up, then gain the cracks by a difficult move left. Continue directly for 15m, then more easily up to the right to a right-angled corner (27m). Quit the corner by bridging on small holds to a terrace (6m). Easier slabs lead to the buttress top at a point some 18m below the top of Waterfall Gully (45m). *Diagram page 142-143.*

167   Harrison's Climb Direct   275m   IV
K. V. Crocket and C. Gilmore   February 1976

Start at the right hand end of the face, below the deep chimney-gully which separates the North Wall of Carn Dearg from Cousins' Buttress.

Two steep pitches, then snow lead to the neck of the buttress. Move left on to the upper section, then from the right end of the large icefall take a rising line right, to the edge overlooking Raeburn's Buttress. Continue for several pitches to the upper coire, from where a selection of routes can be followed to the summit. *Diagram page 142-143.*

168   Baird's Buttress   90m   Very Difficult
P. D. Baird and E. J. A. Leslie   June 1938

This pleasant buttress lies in the rightmost reaches of the upper coire, just before the rocks join the upper section of Raeburn's Buttress.

The start is from an obvious ledge gained from Raeburn's Buttress, or by descending the upper coire from Ledge Route. Follow the crack splitting the front of the buttress in two steep pitches (24m). A steep wall above, then easier climbing leads to the top of the buttress. *Diagram page 142-143.*

RAEBURN'S BUTTRESS

This is the slender, tapering buttress between the main mass of Carn Dearg and The Castle. From some viewpoints the buttress appears almost as a pinnacle.

17 Raeburn's Buttress (Dave Jenkins). *Photo: C. Stead*

169   **Original Route**   230m   Very Difficult
H. Raeburn, H. MacRobert and D. S. Arthur   September 1908

A climb with good situations.

Start up the gully on the left or south side of the buttress and climb easy water-worn rocks for 60m to where the gully bifurcates to form two chimneys. Climb the right branch to a cave and belay (30m). Exit by the right wall and gain a chockstone. Traverse right into a chimney-gully and belay (24m). Follow the gully easily to a pitch giving access to the terrace on the neck of the buttress (30m). Alternatively, traverse right on to the crest of the buttress and climb to the terrace. Climb the crest of the buttress to finish by a vertical step and narrow arete leading to easy ground (85m). *Diagram page 142-143.*

WINTER   **IV**

W. D. Brooker and J. M. Taylor   January 1959

This gives an excellent and sustained climb.

Climb steep snow with short ice pitches to the cave. In easy conditions this gives a 10m ice pitch, otherwise it can be a very awkward verglased problem. Above, follow the grooves or arete depending on the prevailing conditions.

170   **Boomer's Requiem**   170m   IV
C. Higgins and D. McArthur   February 1973

Follow the gully as for the Original Route to the bifurcation. From here the left branch is normally barred by an impressive, steep icefall. Climb this in two pitches to gain the upper slopes. Not shown on diagram.

171   **The Crack**   185m   Very Severe
H. A. Carsten and T. McGuinness   June 1946

This tremendous and neglected climb follows the prominent crack splitting the steep front of the buttress.

From the lower rocks in the introductory gully of the Original Route, scramble up right to the foot of the crack. Access is barred by deceptive, difficult, vegetated slabs which are climbed right to a ledge and block belays (15m). Climb the crack by a series of hard, overhanging pitches to gain easier rock and a junction with the Original Route (70m). Finish as for that route. *Diagram page 142-143.*

172   **Compression Crack**   120m   Very Difficult
C. F. Rolland and H. I. Ogilvy   June 1940

This gives splendid climbing on good, clean rock.

Scramble by easy slabs and grass ledges above the left wall of South Castle Gully (see below) to reach a well defined ledge beneath a chimney-corner, half-way along the steep north wall of Raeburn's Buttress. This ledge may also be gained by a right traverse from the foot of the final arete of the Original Route.

Climb the chimney on clean, waterworn rock in two pitches of 12m and 24m, strenuous and progressively difficult. Above the chimney, break up to the left over slabs to the top of Raeburn's Buttress (36m). *Diagram page 142-143.*

173   **South Castle Gully**   230m   I
W. Brunskill, W. W. King and W. W. Naismith   April 1896

The gully divides Raeburn's Buttress on the left from the buttress of The Castle on the right.

Under normal conditions the gully provides an uncomplicated snow ascent.

Care is required in bad conditions as the rock formation of the gully makes it prone to avalanche. *Diagram page 41 and 142-143.*

THE CASTLE

The buttress rises from an undercut snout, in the form of a slabby wedge topped by a headwall of fine, steep rock, distinctively contained by the divergent North and South Castle Gullies.

174   **Original Route**   230m   Very Difficult
H. Raeburn and T. Gibson   September 1898

Start beneath the undercut nose of the buttress at a slabby break.

Climb overhanging rock on good holds for 4m, ,then more easily to a belay (8m). Continue by scrambling, bearing slightly left to reach a shallow gully which leads to a grass terrace under the upper slabs (120m). Climb the slabs slightly right, then left by an awkward corner and move left into a chimney (21m). Follow this to a chockstone belay (18m). Break out by the right wall, past an awkward corner, then by slabs to a shallow gully which leads to a grass bay and belay (21m). Climb slabs on the right, then a short chimney (12m). More slabs on the right lead to a short wall and the top. *Diagram page 142-143.*

WINTER III

W. Brown, J. Maclay, W. Naismith and G. Thomson   April 1896

A cone of avalanche snow often masks the first pitch making it easy. Steep snow is then followed up the centre of the buttress. Near the top, if the slabs are iced, the climb will present considerable difficulties.

The slabby character of the buttress creates an avalanche tendency and the ascent should not be attempted if such conditions prevail.

175 **The Keep** 75m Severe

J. M. Alexander and I. S. Clough   June 1958

An enjoyable variation on the Original Route.

Climb the Original Route for some 130m to a grass terrace under the upper slabs, then traverse down right to a corner and block belay. Climb above the belay to a ledge, move right and follow a groove to a grass ledge and block belay (15m). Climb on to a projecting block and continue to a good stance and belay (12m). Climb a groove, surmount a bulge and continue to easier climbing and a flake belay (18m). The groove continues, but the slab edge on the left gives a better finish (30m). *Diagram page 142-143.*

176 **North Castle Gully** 230m I

J. H. Bell and R. G. Napier   April 1896

This gully separates The Castle from Castle Ridge.

The gully gives an uncomplicated snow ascent with rarely a large cornice. *Diagram page 41 and 142-143.*

CASTLE RIDGE

This is the last and least difficult of the great ridges on the north face of the mountain, but the ascent has a distinctive quality deriving from the fine views out over Lochaber. The great, broken North Wall has lately yielded a few rock routes and several excellent winter lines.

177 **Castle Ridge**   275m   Moderate

Dr and Mrs Inglis Clark, J. G. Inglis and Rev. J. W. Inglis   May 1899

The ridge is mainly scrambling with a few moderate pitches.

Start at the lowest point of the buttress, over rocks crossed by ledges raking up right, which tend to lead the climber on to the right wall of the buttress. Maintain the direct line by crossing a succession of slabs to gain some huge, detached blocks (90m). Continue by the steeper rocks above to gain an almost level section of the ridge (75m). This point can be gained more easily from the foot of North Castle Gully. The steep rocks above are climbed by a 10m chimney, then more easily to another steep section climbed by a 12m chimney. The ridge now narrows and a steep rib can be climbed by thin cracks, but several routes are possible. The angle above relents and scrambling leads to the top.

An easy descent can be made down the slopes on the right, or north, over an extensive boulder field to the Lochan Meall An t-Suidhe. *Diagram page 41 and 142-143.*

WINTER   III

J. N. Collie, W. W. Naismith, G. Thomson and M. W. Travers   April 1895

The ridge is best gained from below the Castle Gullies. In good conditions it provides a fine winter climb which should always be possible to a competent party. Difficulties are generally turned on the left.

NORTH WALL OF CASTLE RIDGE

The following routes are located on the great, broken North Wall of the Castle Ridge, well seen from the walk up the Allt a'Mhuilinn.

178 **The Serpent**   300m   II

I. S. Clough, D. Pipes and J. Porter   February 1959

A steep snow climb.

Start near the left edge of the face at a small gully above the Luncheon Stone. Climb the gully, then by a shelf curving right to reach the lower section of another gully (150m). Follow this to the shoulder of Carn Dearg. *Diagram page 137.*

18
The North Wall of Castle Ridge of Carn Dearg

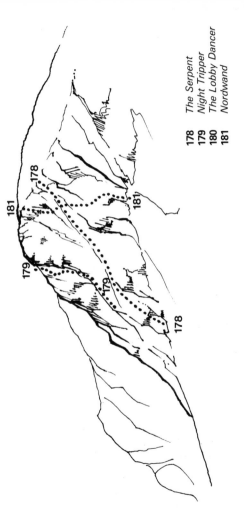

178	The Serpent
179	Night Tripper
180	The Lobby Dancer
181	Nordwand

179 **Night Tripper** 183m Hard Very Severe
N. Muir and R. Schipper September 1971

Start to the right of the great overhang of Castle Ridge at a prominent groove system. The main feature of the climb is the series of square-cut roofs at two-thirds height.

Climb the open groove to a steepening and move out right over an overhang to a belay above, below a short corner (45m). Climb the corner to a glacis, then the cracked, wet wall above to a groove continuation on the left. Step on to this and go up to a large stance beneath the overhangs (40m). Move up the corner 10m until a series of handholds lead left under the roofs, continuing until possible to step left round the overlap onto a slab, then climb trending right to a comfortable stance and belay (45m). Climb a black corner slab on the left to a final corner which is climbed first direct, then left at the top to block belays (43m). Climb up and left to belay on boulder-strewn ledges (10m). *Diagram page 137.*

180 **The Lobby Dancer** 180m V
C. Higgins and A. Kimber February 1977

This line of ascent approximates to Night Tripper and follows the groove system right of the overhanging wall. Access to the climb is either direct by some ice pitches, or from the left using a diagonal ledge line.

Follow the groove in three pitches to belay below a barrier wall. Gain the continuation of the groove above the wall using aid (difficult pegging 10m). Climb to a block belay on the right, then left to finish on the crest of Castle Ridge. *Diagram page 137.*

The groove line to the right of this route gives the line of Alchemist, V (not described).

181 **Nordwand** 425m III
I. S. Clough, D. Pipes, B. Sarll, F. Jones and J. Porter February 1959

An interesting climb.

Start in a small gully near the right edge of the face and climb to an ice pitch. Traverse left to a natural line of ascent which is followed for 215m to a point where the gully of The Serpent comes in from the left. Cross this and climb steep snow for 120m to the foot of the summit rocks. These are climbed by a series of walls and traverses leading to the left to gain the final rocks of Castle Ridge. *Diagram page 137.*

GLEN NEVIS

From the Glen Nevis road, several gullies can be seen etched into the southern flank of Ben Nevis. These, the Glen Nevis gullies offer sport of varying degrees of aquatic interest, but they also include in their ranks what is, without doubt the finest example of their kind, namely Surgeon's Gully.

Its barrier pitch still awaits a direct ascent as does the intriguing central branch, the combination of which would probably produce the longest and most difficult gully climb in the country.

182 Surgeon's Gully   450m   Very Severe
D. H. Haworth and G. Ritchie   August 1947

Start to the right of the old graveyard and follow the gully by small, slabby pitches to the base of a major chockstone pitch.

1. Climb to the cave (18m), exit by a slab on the right.
2. An awkward start, then back and foot to the top of a chockstone, exit on the left (8m).
3. Climb directly for 10m, then back and foot to turn the chockstone by the right wall (18m).
4. The gully is followed with ease to the barrier pitch, a magnificent section over 30m high, with a large chockstone in its upper reaches. Regrettably this is unclimbed and the route goes by the right wall, 10m from the back of the gully.

Climb the vegetated right wall, finishing by an open chimney. Traverse up and left and descend into the gully in a further 30m.

7. Climb a sloping rake on the left on good holds (12m).
8. Chockstone pitch (8m).
9. Waterfall pitch. Start up the left side, traverse right into the waterfall and climb it direct (11m).
10. Chockstone pitch climbed back and foot (6m).
11. and 12. Waterfall pitches of 6m and 8m.
13. Easier angled sloping pitch (8m).
14. This is the hardest pitch. A large chockstone and attendant waterfall block the exit. Start a few metres back on the right wall; climb a smooth groove (delicate). Move right to a stance and runner and continue 3m to a peg belay. Go up 3m, surmount the nose on the left, then traverse left into the waterfall to climb into a cave beneath the exit chockstone. From a good runner, climb the chockstone to a thread belay 8m higher.

15. Climb the rake on the left side (11m).

16. Chockstone, turned on the left with difficulty (11m).

17. The central groove (5m).

18. A smooth groove on the extreme right (5m).

19. Waterfall pitch. Start on the right and work obliquely left into it, then straight up the watercourse from the half-way point (18m).

20. Climb the watercourse to exit by a large chockstone (36m).

21. Climb to the chockstone and turn it on the left (14m).

22. Continue by the bed to the final pitch which has the largest chockstone in the gully. Climb it on the left or right (10m).

This brings one to a horizontal deer track and fence and is the end point of the original ascent. Above, the gully opens out to form three branches. The left is a simple scramble, the central very steep and apparently difficult and the right patently more possible, but both awaiting an ascent!

POLLDUBH CRAGS

Further along Glen Nevis, where the road bridges the river at the lower Falls of Nevis, the Polldubh Crags can be seen near the foot of the southern slopes of the mountain.

They have a frontage of 1km, face south and provide a fine range of climbs on excellent rock and are often in good condition when upper cliffs are not. A further asset is the great scenic beauty of Glen Nevis.

The buttresses are described from left to right as one proceeds up Glen Nevis. Earlier exploration by many groups must account for many unrecorded ascents on these crags. For a definitive reference to these crags, see *Rock Climbs in Glen Nevis* by K. Schwartz and D. S. B. Wright, published by Nevisport. Only a small selection is given here.

SHEEP FANK BUTTRESS

This is the first and leftmost of the small crags and lies about 80m above the road bridge. It is approached from the sheep fank at the car park near the falls, whence a fence line leads to the buttress. *Diagram page 144.*

183 **Gambit** 33m Severe

Climb the raking crack on the left wall of the buttress.

184 **Sheep Fank Wall** 33m Difficult

Start to the right of the overhanging base. Climb by a slab and crack, then follow the crest.

VARIATIONS

Fence Edge 15m Severe

Climb the left side of the buttress above the fence.

Brown Groove 10m Severe

Climb the brown groove on the right of the buttress.

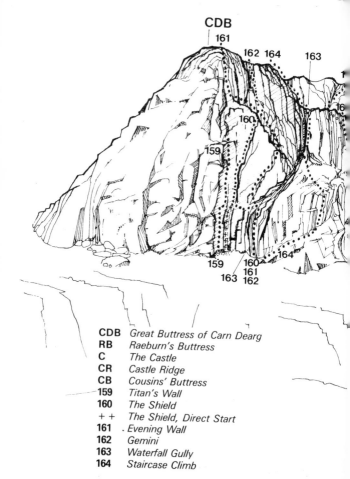

CDB

161

162 164 163

160

159

159 160 164
163 162
161

Dearg to Castle Ridge

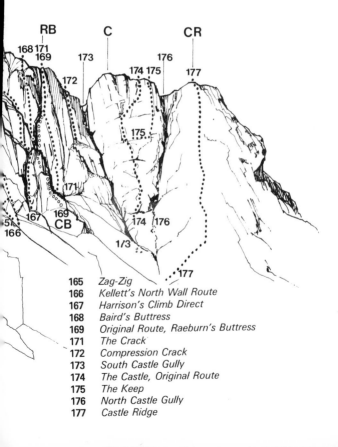

19

Polldubh Crags

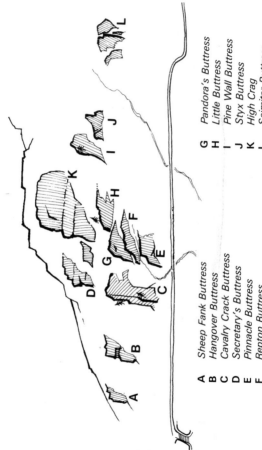

A   Sheep Fank Buttress
B   Hangover Buttress
C   Cavalry Crack Buttress
D   Secretary's Buttress
E   Pinnacle Buttress
F   Repton Buttress

G   Pandora's Buttress
H   Little Buttress
I   Pine Wall Buttress
J   Styx Buttress
K   High Crag
L   Scimitar Buttress

HANGOVER BUTTRESS

This stands above some large boulders about 200m from the bridge. A large overhang is a prominent feature of this buttress. *Diagram page 144.*

185   Route I   33m   Very Difficult

Start at the lowest rocks to climb a rib and continue to a grass ledge. Climb a short wall and traverse right by an awkward corner to finish above the overhang.

186   Route II   30m   Severe

Start left of, and climb directly to, the overhang; traverse beneath it for 6m, then finish by a groove above.

CAVALRY CRACK BUTTRESS

This is located 200m beyond and a little lower than Hangover Buttress. It carries two big pine trees high on the face, has an imposing left wall and is deservedly one of the most popular crags. *Diagram page 144.*

187   The Old Wall   42m   Very Severe

Start under the obvious chimney-crack on the steep left wall of the buttress.

Climb the crack for 10m to just past a small tree. Traverse right and up for 5m to follow a direct, exposed line leading to the right end of the escape ledge on Storm (see below).

188   Storm   92m   Hard Very Severe

Start under the steep left edge of the buttress.

Climb the steep lefthand groove for 6m, then gain the righthand groove and climb to a ledge (30m). Climb a diagonal crack to a prominent pine (27m). Climb a groove right of the pine and finish by a steep wall above to the buttress edge (15m). Finish by a groove on the left (15m).

It is possible to make an escape from the pine by a stomach traverse to the right (Severe).

VARIATION—DIRECT FINISH   25m   Hard Very Severe

A more difficult finish is to climb into the corner above and left of the pine, exit on the left at the overhang, then by steep rock to finish.

189   **Heat Wave**   92m   Very Difficult

Start at the left edge of the buttress.

Climb a groove with a holly tree at its foot for 6m; step left into another groove, then, reaching a tree, climb up to a heather ledge below the diagonal crack of Storm. Traverse right round the corner to a ledge and tree belay below a vegetatious gully. Follow the slabby left wall of the gully to a ledge. Finish by the slabs.

SECRETARY'S BUTTRESS

This is located almost centrally among the crags and above Cavalry Crack Buttress. It is easily identified by the rectangular form and the oblique crack raking to the right across the face. *Diagram page 144.*

190   **Secretary's Crack**   50m   Difficult

Climb the chimney-crack (21m). From its top, traverse left to follow the slab crest of the buttress.

191   **Direct Route**   80m   Severe

Climb the front of the buttress by a smooth slab corner, then by the thin, central crack on the right to the top of Secretary's Crack. Finish by the slabs of that route.

PINNACLE RIDGE

This is situated some 600m from the bridge and about 30m above the road. Its slab face is defined on the left by a steep wall and to the right by overhanging rock. *Diagram page 144.*

192   **Original Route**   45m   Very Difficult

Climb from the lowest rocks to a small tree above the vertical crack in the left wall. Continue by a slab basin; traverse right by a large flake and ascend the final slabs direct.

VARIATIONS

Climb the vertical crack in the left wall, strenuous and Severe (6m).
Climb the left of two parallel cracks, Very Severe (8m).
Climb the wall left of the parallel cracks, trending left over the final bulge, Extremely Severe (15m).
Climb the slabs to the right of the introductory pitch, Severe (6m).

REPTON BUTTRESS

Viewed from the road, the buttress lies just behind Pinnacle Ridge and is in the form of a long ridge, leading up from left to right above a wall, marked by rounded overhangs on the right. *Diagram page 144.*

193 **Three Pines**   30m   Severe

Start near the middle of the face and climb the rib to the pines (18m). Climb the groove behind the middle tree, then right under the roof to a platform and finish by a crack.

PANDORA'S BUTTRESS

This is the second buttress above the Pinnacle Ridge, immediately left of and above Repton Buttress and 90m right of Cavalry Crack Buttress. *Diagram page 144.*

194 **Phantom Slab**   40m   Very Severe

Start at the foot of a rib left of, and 22m above the lowest rocks.
Climb the rib edge (15m). Traverse right, gain the slab above a step, or by the groove to the tree belay (20m). Climb the superb slab on the left (20m).

195 **Flying Dutchman**   60m   Severe

Start at the righthand of the lowest rocks.
Climb the ridge crest to a grass terrace and tree belay. Climb the slabs on the left to traverse left under the overhang, cross this on the left and climb direct to a tree belay. Follow the ridge to finish.
An excellent climb.

LITTLE BUTTRESS

Situated above and to the right of Pandora's Buttress, its front is divided at mid-height by a ledge with a large pine tree above the left end. *Diagram page 144.*

196 Spike   58m   Very Difficult

Start near some boulders and climb clean slabs on the front of the buttress to a tree. Continue up, then traverse to the buttress edge, stance and belay above. Finish by the slab above.

PINE WALL BUTTRESS

This is about 60m above the Pinnacle Buttress and some 200m to its right. It is probably best approached by following the burn left of Pinnacle Ridge to its source where the buttress can be identified as a prominent ridge with a large pine on top of its second tier. *Diagram page 144.*

197 Pine Wall   67m   Very Difficult

Start at the lowest point and climb to gain a corner leading to a platform (12m). Continue up left over a bulge, then by slabs just right of the rounded crest (30m). Follow the ridge or grooves to the pine for 14m, pass an overhang on the left, then just left of the crest to finish (21m).

198 The Gutter   45m   Difficult

Start 4m right of Pine Wall and climb twin cracks to a ledge. Continue by the deep crack above to finish by the ridge leading to the pine.

STYX BUTTRESS

This fine crag is situated immediately right of Pine Wall Buttress. It is steep with several overhangs. *Diagram page 144.*

199 Ascension   30m   Hard Very Severe

Climb the oblique chimney on the lower reaches of the left wall, to follow the lower of two diagonal cracks to a slanting ledge. Continue the line over a bulge to a little tree, then by an overhung groove to finish.

200   **Resurrection**   35m   Very Severe

Follow the long, tapering slab up the left side of the buttress. The difficulty is sustained.

201   **Damnation**   28m   Very Severe

Start 6m right of the central edge of the buttress. Climb a ramp to a little pine, traverse right to climb a vertical rib and the overhang above. Finish by the fine slab above to a tree.

HIGH CRAG

This is the large, tiered buttress high up and to the right of Secretary's Crack Buttress, above and to the left of Pine Wall Buttress. *Diagram page 144.*

202   **Crag Lough Grooves**   140m   Hard Very Severe

The route ascends the left front of the buttress. Start to the left of a cave overhang at the foot.

Climb a small corner to belay beneath overhangs (12m). Traverse right over ribs for 3m, to enter a groove and climb this to a heather ledge (23m). Follow slabs above to a large terrace (40m). Climb to and traverse right along a prominent gangway to turn a corner and reach a small stance (18m). Climb the shallow groove and slabs above to a grass ledge (21m). Finish by slabs (36m).

203   **Cervix**   30m   Very Severe

Start from the gully bounding High Crag on the left, at the base of its middle tier.

Climb a 10m wall by a left raking crack, then the steep, slanting chimney above.

SCIMITAR BUTTRESS

This is the middle of three buttresses some 300m to the right of Pinnacle Ridge. It is about 100m above the road bend and has a sharp pinnacle at its base. *Diagram page 144.*

18 Damnation (Ed Jackson). *Photo: C. Stead*

204 **Nutcracker Chimney**   23m   Severe

The obvious chimney on the left of the buttress.

205 **Wanderlust**   35m   Very Difficult

Take the right hand of two slanting cracks on the right of the
buttress. Climb to its end, then traverse left and up to finish.

K

BINNEIN SHUAS

Binnein Shuas, G.R. 827 463, is situated in the Ardverikie Forest, east of Loch Laggan and is very attractively placed, overlooking Lochan na h-Earba. The most useful maps to the area are the O.S. Second Series sheet 34, or the One Inch sheet 36.

ACCESS AND APPROACHES

Access is gained from the A86 Spean Bridge to Newtonmore road at a concrete bridge, approximately 1km west of the west end of Loch Laggan. Cars are not permitted across this bridge. Cross the bridge and follow the estate road, going left at the first fork and negotiating a locked gate. Continue on the wide road to its junction with a narrower road on the right. Take the narrow road which contours round the south-west end of Binnein Shuas, keeping to the left past an unnamed lochan, to reach the much larger Lochan na h-Earba (¾ hour). The cliffs are now visible up on the left, overlooking the west side of the Lochan and can be reached in a further 20 minutes.

This area is a deer forest and access is not allowed during the stalking season which extends from 12th August to 20th October.

ACCOMMODATION

There is a small campsite at the south west end of Lochan na h-Earba.

MOUNTAIN RESCUE

For rescue services, contact the Police by dialling 999. There is a public telephone box near Moy Lodge, at the west end of Loch Laggan.

THE CLIMBING

The cliffs face east. The rock is mostly clean and sound, but is greasy when wet. Some of the routes, especially those on the East Sector are slow to dry. This is a summer crag only and its development has been relatively recent, most of the climbs having been pioneered by D. F. Lang and G. N. Hunter, after a brief foray by Tom Patey.

The cliffs are described in two sectors, West and East, separated from each other by Hidden Gully. The West sector is the lefthand section of crag. Its right extremity, which stretches furthest down the hillside, has some very big and prominent overhangs. This part is known as the Fortress. Left of this, the rocks extend leftwards (west) up the hillside, diminishing in height as they rise. Hidden Gully is well named and is only obvious from below. It runs up and left and contains some chockstone pitches of Very Difficult standard. It gives a poor winter climb of Grade III standard.

The right wall of Hidden Gully marks the start of the East Sector, that part immediately right of the gully foot being known as Ardverikie Wall. The East Sector is divided by a terrace into two tiers, the lower of which is short, broken and vegetated and of little climbing interest, although a 45m Very Severe, Whiplash, has been recorded. One pitch from the top of the East Sector is another terrace, the line of which also extends across the West Sector. The main part of the East Sector stretches a long way right from Hidden Gully and although there is much rock, it is less attractive looking than the West Sector and the Ardverikie Wall area, being smoother, with a horizontal stratification and more vegetation. Nevertheless, the climbs which are described are very good.

Below and left of Hidden Gully and well below the West Sector, is a small, slabby face, on which are three short (45m) and pleasant routes from Very Difficult to Very Severe.

THE WEST SECTOR

The climbs are described from right to left.

206   The Fortress Direct   166m   Hard Very Severe
Upper part: *T. W. Patey, R. Ford and Mary Stewart   May 1964*
Lower part: *R. Carrington and J. R. Marshall   July 1970*

This route climbs the right edge of the Fortress and, despite its appearance, gives fine sustained climbing.

Start at the lowest rocks of the West Sector, just left of Hidden Gully, at a mossy groove with an overhang. Climb the groove, entering from the right, turn the overhang on the left and continue to a terrace (40m). Climb twin cracks above to a second terrace (15m) and go up to a belay (30m). Traverse out right to a triangular, overhanging niche with a steep crack rising from its roof. Climb this fine crack, step right at the top and climb to a big ledge (30m). Climb the edge in two pitches to finish (66m). *Diagram page 158.*

VARIATION START   30m

Of similar standard to the original, but much better. Start up and right of the mossy groove at the foot of a clean groove with a big roof, low down. Climb to the roof, avoid by a left layback and continue up the groove to the first stance of the original route. *Diagram page 158.*

207 **The Keep** 114m   Hard Very Severe
D. F. Lang and G. N. Hunter   July 1967

This follows the left edge of the Fortress, i.e. the left edge of the overhung section. Originally climbed with two points of aid, it now goes free.

Scramble to gain a grassy ramp with a rowan tree. Above, is a crack in the left wall. Climb the crack to a stance (12m). Continue by grooves on the buttress edge to two steep cracks. Climb using both of these and follow the fault above, passing a loose block to gain a slab and so to a belay (30m). Climb slabs to the top in two pitches (27m and 45m). *Diagram page 158.*

208 **Kubla Khan** 111m   Severe
D. F. Lang and G. N. Hunter   June 1967

This route is on the slabby left wall of the Fortress, starting just right of a prominent dyke. The pale white slab of pitch two is very striking.

Climb a steep grooved wall to a grass ledge right of the dyke (18m). Climb the pale grooved slab until moves left lead to a recess and belay at 42m (a superb pitch). Go straight up to a terrace (12m). Climb an overhang by the big boulder and the easy lichenous slabs above (39m). *Diagram page 158.*

209 **Cube Wall** 117m   Severe
D. F. Lang and G. N. Hunter   September 1967

Start left of Kubla Khan, at the left side of the prominent dyke, a few metres right of a rock scar and well down and right of a broken gully.

Climb a crack in a thin corner to a ledge on the left and move left along small ledges to a diagonal fault which runs up right. (This point can be gained more directly by climbing the rock scar.) Climb the fault and the upper part of a big corner to a ledge and belay (36m). Take the wall above to a terrace (21m). From the top of the large boulder on the right, gain the slabs above and climb these, at first rightwards by a groove and then direct to the top (60m, belays scarce). *Diagram page 158.*

210 **Blaeberry Grooves** 75m   Very Severe
D. F. Lang and G. N. Hunter   September 1967

This lies up the imposing, central crackline on the steep face near the top of the line of crags forming the West Sector. This face lies below

19 Fortress Direct, Variation Start (Alan Kennedy).

Photo: C. Stead

20 Kubla Khan, pitch two (Andy Matthews). *Photo: C. Stead*

and right of a wet black wall and left of the broken gully to the left of Cube Wall.

Climb the central cracks to a ledge (30m). Gain the slab above and follow the easy central crack to the top in 45m. *Diagram page 158.*

Right of Blaeberry Grooves is a wider, tapering crack line. This is the line of Gorgon, Hard Very Severe.

THE EAST SECTOR

This is the area right of Hidden Gully. The climbs here are described from left to right, starting with those routes which begin on the right wall of Hidden Gully.

211 **Flypaper** 111m Very Severe
D. F. Lang and G. N. Hunter June 1967

To begin this route, climb Hidden Gully for some 60m to where it narrows.

Climb a steep red wall on the right, on small holds and go over a small overhang to a little birch tree in a corner. Short of the tree, go rightwards to a ledge and belay (39m). Traverse horizontally left for 8m, then up for 10m and left to a terrace (27m). Climb a prominent red streak above to a flake runner. leave the flake on small holds to reach a layback crack which is followed to the top (45m). *Diagram page 158 and 160.*

212 **Hurricane** 153m Very Severe
C. Ogilvie and Miss C. Stock September 1976

This lies on the right wall of Hidden Gully and starts 6m below its first step at a rock scar. A rowan tree is visible on the wall above.

Climb a shallow corner right of the rock scar, continuing by a faint groove to gain the ledge, just left of the tree. Move up left to a higher tree on a ledge (39m). Move right and climb a rib (junction with Usquebaugh) to a belay below an overhang (24m). Step right onto the slab and climb it directly to the overhang and go right to a ledge (18m). Go back down left and climb the overhang and fine slab above, direct to the terrace and a flake belay (30m). Climb the slab above (42m). *Diagram page 158 and 160.*

20 The West Sector of Binnein Shuas and Part of the East Sector

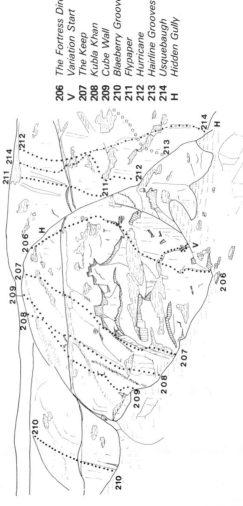

206 The Fortress Direct
V   Variation Start
207 The Keep
208 Kubla Khan
209 Cube Wall
210 Blaeberry Grooves
211 Flypaper
212 Hurricane
213 Hairline Grooves
214 Usquebaugh
H   Hidden Gully

213   Hairline Grooves   120m   Severe
D. F. Lang and G. N. Hunter   September 1967

This route takes a thin crack line across Ardverikie Wall.

Start 15m up Hidden Gully, at a pink waterworn fault on its right wall, below and right of the rock scar of Hurricane. Climb the fault, passing left of a spike at 6m. Continue past the spike, then traverse right 3m to a faint line of cracks which lead to black rocks and a grass ledge. Belay at the white scar beyond (27m). From the right side of the scar, trend up right to a crack which overlooks Ardverikie Wall. Climb the crack, through a small overlap, until a right traverse leads to the big flake belay on pitch 3 of Ardverikie Wall (36m). Step off the belay flake and follow the thin crack up right to a good thread belay (39m). Easy climbing leads to the top in 18m. *Diagram page 158 and 160.*

214   Usquebaugh   168m   Severe
G. N. Hunter and D. F. Lang   June 1968

Start at the red waterworn streak on the right wall of Hidden Gully at its foot. Climb a short crack on the right to a grass ledge and continue by the corner on the left to a white rock scar and peg belay (42m). Climb the staircase behind the belay and the rib above to belay below an overhang (42m). Break through the overlapping corner on the left, to follow a sloping corner and a slab to the terrace and move left to belay at a block (42m). Climb the short overhang behind the belay, continue by a steep slab to a scoop and take the rib on its left to the top (42m). *Diagram page 158 and 160.*

215   Ardverikie Wall   160m   Severe
D. F. Lang and G. N. Hunter   June 1967

A splendid classic route on perfect rock and easy for its grade. It takes a direct line up the face, right of Hidden Gully and starts 8m left of a boulder which forms an arch.

Climb a rib and a short corner to a niche (15m). Regain the rib on the left and climb it to a slab. Trend right, then left to a ledge and flake belay (3̶6̶m̶)̶ ✱ Move right from the belay to holds (crux), then slightly left up an ill-defined rib and shallow left-trending groove to belay below a large scoop (33m). Climb the left side of the scoop and cross the overlap to a slab leading to the terrace (16m). Finish up easy slabs. Harder and more direct variations may be made. *Diagram page 160.*

✱ CLIMB SLAB & OVERLAP TO FLAKE BELAY (30M)

216   Soft Shoe Shuffle   82m   Very Severe
G. N. Hunter and D. F. Lang   May 1968

This fine climb is on the steep, clean wall, some 90m right of Ardverikie Wall.

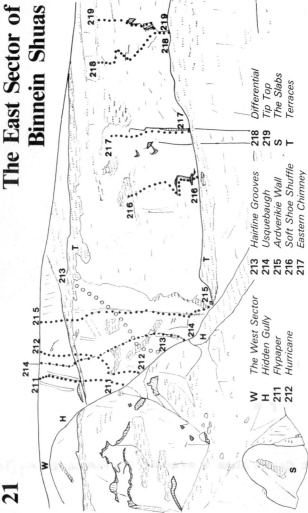

The East Sector of Binnein Shuas

21

W   The West Sector
H   Hidden Gully
211 Flypaper
212 Hurricane
213 Hairline Grooves
214 Usquebaugh
215 Ardverikie Wall
216 Soft Shoe Shuffle
217 Eastern Chimney
218 Differential
219 Tip Top
S   The Slabs
T   Terraces

21 Usquebaugh, final pitch (Pete Moffat). *Photo: C. Stead*

22 Differential, pitch one (Alan Kennedy). *Photo: C. Stead*

Start at a cairn on a flat slab, below an overhang. Climb the overhang by moving in from the right above it, to climb a crack to a ledge and flake belay (13m). Traverse left below an overhang for 8m to a break which is climbed on loose blocks. Move right to a ledge and peg belay (12m). Climb a corner on the right, then go diagonally right by a line of flakes to a small stance and flake belay at the left side of a slab (18m). Go up left to climb a steep white quartz band directly, over several bulges to a block belay (39m). Scramble to the top. *Diagram page 160.*

217 Eastern Chimney 75m Severe
J. McDowell and D. Todd   May 1969

This excellent climb is the righthand of the two prominent chimneys, well along to the right from Ardverikie Wall, just before the crag bends in to the right to form an angle.

Climb the chimney to a grass ledge (33m). Continue in the chimney until a move left leads to a corner which is followed to a short wall and the top. *Diagram page 160.*

The chimney to the left of this gives the line of Second Prize, Hard Severe.

218 Differential 75m Very Severe
J. McDowell and D. Todd   May 1969

This and the following climb start at the same point, some 70m right of Eastern Chimney. Look for a huge block 6m high, which is 10m above the ground. The block is bounded on its left by a prominent, black, lichenous corner. A turfy groove leads to the foot of this corner. From this groove, climb diagonally left past a grass pocket at 18m, until a slab leads to a left traverse to an obvious groove. Climb the groove, continuing diagonally right past a shelf overhang to a belay. Go left, until an easy chimney leads to the top. *Diagram page 160.*

219 Tip Top 80m Very Severe
J. McDowell and D. Todd   May 1969

Start as Differential. Climb the turfy groove to the foot of the black corner and move up and right onto the face of the block, which is climbed, finishing by a nasty move to a grass ledge. Belay in a corner onthe right (27m). Climb the corner, traversing the right wall after 15m to an arete, which leads to a belay (23m). Continue directly to the top. *Diagram page 160.*

CREAG MEAGHAIDH

Creag Meaghaidh (pronounced "Meggie"), 1,128m, G.R. 876 418, is situated north of Loch Laggan, in the Moy Forest. The most useful map of the area is the O.S. Second Series, sheet 34. Creag Meaghaidh offers in Coire Ardair, on its eastern flank, some of the finest winter climbing in Scotland.

ACCESS

Creag Meaghaidh is easily gained from any of the major Scottish cities via the main A86 Spean Bridge to Newtonmore road.

There are no restrictions on winter access.

ACCOMMODATION

Permission to camp in the area may be obtained from Aberarder Farm. There is a primitive damp howff under a large boulder, below the Pinnacle Buttress. Bunkhouse accommodation is available at Fersit, some distance west of Loch Laggan. The bothy at Aberarder, like that at Laggan Inn, is no longer available.

MOUNTAIN RESCUE

Aberarder Farm at the foot of the approach path is an official Mountain Rescue Post. Additionally, a stretcher and basic equipment is stored in the small hut at the north-east corner of Lochan a' Choire Ardair, where the approach path reaches the Lochan.

APPROACHES

The climbs in Coire Ardair are well east of the summit of Creag Meaghaidh. The initial approach is made from the A86 road, at the track to Aberarder Farm. There is a convenient lay-by for parking cars some 100m east of the farm track.

Take the track to the farm, passing through a gate just east of the buildings and continue by a path which eventually crosses the burn, to gain and follow the right, or north side of the Allt Coire Ardair. The path stays well above and parallel to the burn. The glen followed takes a great curve to the left, or west, at which point the cliffs come into view. The path eventually descends to the floor of the glen, about 1½km before the Lochan a' Choire Ardair and continues to reach the north-east corner of the Lochan, at the small hut containing the rescue equipment. The total distance is about 7km and takes 1½ to 2 hours under normal conditions. In heavy snow, the path may be obliterated and progress then becomes very laborious and time-consuming.

From the Lochan, a panoramic view of the cliffs may be had.

THE CLIMBING

Coire Ardair provides worthwhile winter climbing only. The rock is a vegetatious and shattered schist, on which, to date, no good rock climbing has been found.

Being centrally situated in Scotland, Creag Meaghaidh tends to suffer the worst weather of both east and west. It is particularly prone to sudden thaws and consequent avalanche danger.

From Lochan a' Choire Ardair, most of the climbing is visible. From left to right, the major faces are: Bellevue Buttress, rounded and situated high on the left and separated from the magnificent, towering Pinnacle Buttress by the left-trending line of Raeburn's Gully. Right of Pinnacle Buttress are the gentler slopes of Easy Gully, above which rises the Post Face with its four great gullies, or Posts. A prominent feature of Bellevue Buttress. Pinnacle Buttress and the Post Face is a virtually continuous ledge line traversing them in their upper half. This gives the line of the unique Creag Meaghaidh Girdle Traverse. This line, to some extent, detracts from the seriousness of the main routes, as it provides a possible escape.

Right of the Post Face, the crags turn in to form the Inner Coire, whose features are not clearly distinguished from the Lochan. The Inner Coire terminates at the Window, the name given to the very prominent bealach between Creag Meaghaidh on the left and Stob Poite Coire Ardair, 1,055m (unnamed on the O.S. map), to the right.

The cliffs will be described from left to right.

WINTER DESCENTS

The summit plateau of Creag Meaghaidh is very flat and featureless, and great care is necessary when navigating on it in poor visibility. Many climbers have been benighted, or have inadvertently descended to Glen Roy. In good conditions, descent by Raeburn's Gully, or Easy Gully is feasible. The ridge of Sron a' Ghoire, which leads back to Aberarder, may also be used and would be the easiest descent from the Bellevue Buttress, or Pinnacle Buttress area in poor conditions. Otherwise, descent is best made by the Window, which leads to the Inner Coire and so to the Lochan.

HISTORY

In April 1896, the formidable team of W. Tough, H. Raeburn and W. Douglas attempted the line of the Centre Post. They were the first to be seriously avalanched there, escaping battered, but unbowed, and suggesting that Post Mortem was almost a more appropriate name. The locals were much taken with their ice axes, one worthy commenting that "they reminded him of a theologist who used to go on the hills wi' a thing like that an' pick oot the ferns wi' it, roots an' a'."

In October 1896, Raeburn climbed the gully named after him.

The cliffs thereafter remained unpopular, only dedicated gardeners like J. H. B. Bell recording rock climbs like Pinnacle Buttress, North Post and the Central Pillar. However, Bell at least realised the winter potential of the mountain and made winter ascents of Staghorn Gully with C. M. Allan, H. M. Kelly and H. Cooper in 1934, followed by the South Pipe with Miss V. Roy in 1935, and finally the Centre Post with Allan in 1937. On an earlier attempt on the latter route, Bell is said to have been armed with a sackful of pitons made from stair rods.

After a further long gap, the South Post fell to N. S. Tennant and C. G. M. Slessor in 1956. This was the start of the golden years, and that great pioneer Tom Patey made much of the opportunities, recording many fine routes including the Last and North Posts, and culminating in his remarkable solo ascent of the Girdle Traverse, J. R. Marshall too, made his mark with the 1959 Face Route and Smith's Gully, named after Robin Smith. Twenty years later, this remains the hardest climb on the mountain and indeed, one of the hardest of the Scottish ice gullies. In 1964, the huge icefall of Centre Post Direct, which had repelled many previous attempts, was climbed by B. Robertson and party.

Throughout the 60s, the Inner Coire was developed, with Patey being particularly active. The best lines however, fell to the Dundee climbers, Pumpkin to N. Quinn, G. S. Peet and R. S. McMillan, and The Wand to Quinn, D. F. Lang, G. N. Hunter and Q. T. Crichton.

The 70s have brought little of real note, but probably the best has yet to come.

BELLEVUE BUTTRESS

This is the furthest left, or east of the buttresses, as one looks from the Lochan. Although a few climbs have been done here, only the following route is recommended.

220   **Eastern Corner**   300m   III
C. G. M. Slessor and K. Bryan   January 1961

At its lowest rocks, Bellevue Buttress is separated by a deep corner from the small buttress on its right. This corner gives the line of the route. It is the most accessible route in the Coire. The first 150m provide interesting climbing, thereafter 150m of steep snow lead to the plateau and possible cornice difficulties. *Diagram page 174-175.*

221   **Raeburn's Gully**   360m   I
H. Raeburn, C. Walker and H. Walker   October 1896

This leftward-sloping gully bounds the left side of Pinnacle Buttress. It gives a straightforward ascent on snow, with variation possible after the first 150m. It also gives access to Ritchie's and Smith's Gullies. *Diagram page 174-175.*

PINNACLE BUTTRESS

Pinnacle Buttress is the great buttress between Raeburn's Gully on the left and Easy Gully on the right. It has a broad frontal face, tapering towards Easy Gully and a steep face which forms the right wall of Raeburn's Gully. The summit tower of the buttress is bounded on its right by a prominent gully which rises from the central snow patches. The steep Raeburn's Gully face has three parallel slits rising from the middle section of Raeburn's Gully. From top to bottom, these are the lines of Ritchie's Gully, Smith's Gully and an unclimbed line. Crossing this section of the face are three ledge lines; that traversing the upper third from Raeburn's Gully is Appolyon Ledge, II, very exposed. That which is gained from Smith's Gully and tapers away before reaching it, is Vanishing Ledge, IV. The lowest line, which slants up from the snow fan at the foot of Raeburn's Gully is Raeburn's Ledge which is not a separate winter route.

The climbs are described from left to right. The first two routes are gained from the middle part of Raeburn's Gully.

222   **Ritchie's Gully**   165m   IV
Upper section: *J. R. Marshall and G. J. Ritchie   February 1957*
Lower Section: G. N. Hunter and N. Quinn   March 1969

This is the leftmost of the three parallel slits on the Raeburn's Gully Face.

L

23 Ritchie's Gully Direct, first winter ascent (Neil Quinn).

Photo: G. N. Hunter

The snow build-up affects the length of the lower part of the climb. Begin at an icefall and climb this, turning an overhang by a right traverse and continuing up to Appolyon Ledge. Climb the gully to the top. The cornice can be difficult. The lower part can be avoided by traversing right along Appolyon ledge. *Diagram page 174-175.*

223   Smith's Gully   180m   V
J. R. Marshall and G. Tiso   February 1959

The central gully of the three on the Raeburn's Gully face. It gives a tremendous climb, but is not often in condition. Climb the gully and its continuation beyond Appolyon Ledge. *Diagram page 174-175.*

224   Nordwander   300m   IV
D. Dinwoodie, B. Lawrie, M. Freeman and D. Stuart   March 1972

Starting near the foot of Raeburn's Gully, this route takes a diagonal line right, across the front face of Pinnacle Buttress, to finish by the prominent ice gully, right of the summit tower of the buttress.

Begin at the snow fan near the foot of Raeburn's Gully, where Raeburn's Ledge slants up right. Traverse the Ledge for one pitch, then break through the walls above to easier iced grooves which lead to the central snow patches and so to the upper gully (junction with 1959 Face Route). Climb the gully to the neck of the buttress. *Diagram page 174-175.*

225   1959 Face Route   450m   IV
J. R. Marshall, J. Stenhouse and D. Haston   February 1959

A magnificent climb on mixed ground, with exciting situations. Towards the right end of the front face of Pinnacle Buttress, some way right of Raeburn's Gully, is a small bay. From the bay, a depression becomes an icy chimney. The route breaks out of this chimney, to head leftwards to a chimney-groove line which leads to the central snow patches and the foot of the prominent gully to the right of the summit tower of the buttress.

Climb 60m up the depression and chimney, break left for 60m to the foot of the second chimney-groove, and climb this, over a big chockstone, to gain the central snow patches in 90m. Go up left to the foot of the prominent gully with its barrier icefall and climb this to finish. *Diagram page 174-175.*

THE POST FACE

The Post Face stretches from Easy Gully on the left, to Staghorn Gully on the right, where the angle is formed as the cliffs turn in to form the Inner Coire. Its most prominent features are the four parallel slits of the Posts, separated by big buttresses. As Easy Gully rises, the Post Face diminishes in height. The Last Post is the leftmost and the North Post the furthest right of the four gullies. From the foot of the right-bounding buttress of the North Post, two parallel shelves slant up right to the foot of two smaller gullies, the Pipes.

This face is very prone to avalanche.

The climbs are described from left to right.

226 **Easy Gully**   450m   I
W. Tough, W. Douglas and H. Raeburn   April 1896

This is the easiest route in the Coire. It lies right of Pinnacle Buttress and slopes up left under the Post Face. The lower part of the gully is narrow, but it widens in its upper section and variations on the left are possible. In descent, keep well out from the Post Face initially, and cut back in below it at mid-height. *Diagram page 174-175.*

227 **The Last Post**   240m   IV/V
T. W. Patey and F. R. Brooke   March 1962

A fine climb.

This is the leftmost of the Posts and starts as an impressive icefall, halfway up Easy Gully. On the first ascent, the left side of the icefall was climbed. Above this, a snowfield steepened to a second icefall, climbed on the right side in two pitches. Easy snow then led to another 30m icefall, avoided by a shelf on the left which led to easier ground below the plateau. Nowadays, the icefalls are usually climbed direct, with a consequent increase in standard. *Diagram page 174-175.*

228 **The South Pillar**   250m   IV
R. Carrington and A. Rouse   Date unknown

Climb the buttress between the Last and South Posts. The exact line is not known. *Diagram page 174-175.*

24 Last Post.

Photo: C. Stead

25 South Post Direct (Alan Pettit). *Photo: C. Stead*

229   **The South Post**   400m   III

N. S. Tennant and C. G. M. Slessor   March 1962

An excellent climb. This is the second Post from the left.

The initial steep icefall is avoided by traversing up and left from the foot of the Centre Post, to gain the gully above the icefall. Climb the couloir above, with one ice pitch, to the foot of a big, steep ice pitch. This is avoided on the left and the gully line regained and followed, with one more ice pitch, to the plateau. *Diagram page 174-175.*

THE SOUTH POST DIRECT   IV

1st Pitch: *T. W. Patey and F. R. Brooke   March 1962*
3rd Pitch: *I. A. MacEacheran and J. Knight   March 1964*

Climb the first and third pitches directly. *Diagram page 174-175.*

230   **The Central Pillar**   400m   IV

T. W. Patey and K. Smith   January 1955

This is the buttress between the South and Centre Posts. It is a good climb and, like the other Pillars, an alternative to the Posts when conditions are poor.

Climb a steep pitch to a snowfield and follow the left side of the buttress to the prominent right-sloping ledge at 250m. The 30m edge forming the right edge of the wall above is climbed, then a snowfield right of the crest, before crossing left and finishing left of the final bulge. *Diagram page 174-175.*

231   **The Centre Post**   400m   III

C. M. Allan and J. H. B. Bell   March 1937

This is the third Post from the left. Its central couloir section is most distinctive. The lower 250m is a steep snowfield which leads, with one ice pitch, to the foot of an impressive icefall. Turn this on the right, by making a steep and airy traverse up the right wall to gain a snowfield, then back left, round a rock outcrop to rejoin the main gully. Much variation is possible after the traverse. Continue up the rest of the gully without further difficulty. *Diagram page 174-175.*

THE CENTRE POST DIRECT   IV/V

B. W. Robertson, F. Harper and E. Cairns   March 1964

Climb the big icefall directly. *Diagram page 174-175.*

PINNACLE BUTTRESS

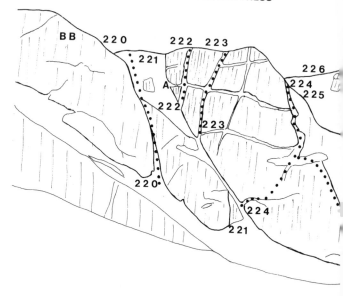

POST FACE

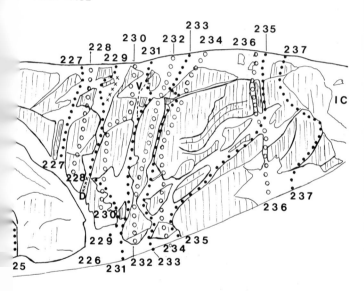

231	*The Centre Post*	
V	*The Centre Post Direct*	
232	*The North Pillar*	
233	*The North Post*	
234	*Easter Pillar*	
235	*Staghorn Gully*	

236	*The South Pipe Direct*
237	*Tresspass Buttress*
A	*Appolyon Ledge*
BB	*Bellevue Buttress*
IC	*The Inner Coire*

232   The North Pillar   400m   IV
A. McKeith and A. N. Other   March 1965

This is the buttress between the Centre and North Posts. It is climbed directly. *Diagram page 174-175.*

233   The North Post   400m   V
T. W. Patey, J. H. Deacon, G. K. McLeod and P. Danelet   February 1960

This is the rightmost and narrowest of the Posts. While providing an excellent climb, it is rarely in climbable condition.

Steep snow leads to a narrow chute and a chockstone pitch. Where the gully widens, a vertical chimney in the left corner gives access to an easy ledge leading to a large platform on the right. Re-cross the terminal face overlooking the gully, by an exposed 25m traverse. A further 30m, first right, then back left, leads to an easy open couloir and the top. *Diagram page 174-175.*

234   Easter Pillar   400m   IV
D. F. Lang and N. Quinn   March 1975

This is the large buttress on the right of the North Post.

Start at its lowest point and climb the left side of the buttress by easy ground for the first 90m, until the buttress steepens. After a further 200m, a right traverse leads along a prominent ledge, then back left and more easily to the top. *Diagram page 174-175.*

Right of Easter Pillar, on the same buttress, lies The Great Buttress, IV, which follows a line some 60m right of the North Post, on the steep, upper section of the buttress.

235   Staghorn Gully   400m   III
C. M. Allan, J. H. B. Bell, H. M. Kelly and H. Cooper   April 1934

An excellent and popular climb.

It is normally approached by the long, partially hidden shelf which slants right, up the angle between the Post Face and the Inner Coire, starting right of the foot of the North Post. This is the lower and more distinct of the two shelves. The shelf is followed to the foot of two parallel gullies, separated by a narrow pillar. These are the two Pipes, that on the left being the South Pipe and on the right, the North Pipe. Continue by the line of the North Pipe, which is the easier of the two. It leads by short pitches to a snow bowl below the plateau. *Diagram page 174-175.*

236 **The South Pipe Direct** 250m IV
South Pipe: *J. H. B. Bell and Miss V. Roy January 1935*
Direct Start: *T. W. Patey and J. H. Deacon February 1960*

Taken together, the South Pipe and the Direct Start to Staghorn Gully give a fine, sustained climb. They are less often in condition.

Begin well up and right of the foot of the shelf of the ordinary start of Staghorn Gully, at an ill-defined gully leading up to the foot of the Pipes. Climb this and the South Pipe directly. *Diagram page 174-175.*

THE INNER COIRE

The Inner Coire stretches from Staghorn Gully to the Window. The climbs here are mostly shorter than those on the other faces. Its main features, from left to right, are firstly a big buttress, Trespass Buttress, a deep ice corner, The Pumpkin, then a narrow gully leading to the twin icefalls of The Wand and Diadem. Right of this, lie broken rocks with a central snowfield, bounding the left side of a gully, Cinderella. Two further gullies cut the rocks between Cinderella and the Window.

The climbs are described from left to right.

237 **Trespass Buttress** 300m IV
G. N. Hunter, H. McInnes, D. F. Lang and N. Quinn March 1969

This interesting climb goes up the buttress with the prominent, narrow chimney, to the right of South Pipe Direct.

Start from a shelf at the foot of South Pipe Direct and climb to gain the chimney. Climb this to a belay by a large overhang. Traverse right to a springboard. Continue up easy ground to the foot of a large chimney, traverse left to the crest of the upper buttress and follow it to where it tapers into the face. Climb a small chimney to easier ground and the top. *Diagram page 174-175.*

238 **The Pumpkin** 300m IV/V
R. McMillan, G. S. Peet and N. Quinn April 1968

The longest and most serious of the Inner Coire routes and rapidly becoming a classic. It comes into condition for long periods most winters. It climbs the long ice corner, right of Trespass Buttress. Climb the 90m corner in two or three pitches to easier ground. Some 45m higher, a steep, left-sloping chimney with an awkward bulge is climbed. Pleasant easy climbing then leads to the top. *Diagram page 179.*

239 **The Sash** 240m II

T. W. Patey, R. W. P. Barclay, M. Laverty and E. Attfield   March 1963

This is a pleasant route which is often in condition.

Start in the narrow gully which leads up to the two parallel icefalls, in the centre of the cliffs. Below the icefalls, a line of shelves lead up and left to the plateau. *Diagram page 179.*

240 **The Wand** 210m IV/V

Q. T. Crichton, D. F. Lang, G. N. Hunter and N. Quinn   February 1969

This is the lefthand of the prominent, twin icefalls. It provides difficult and sustained climbing.

Climb the snow gully of The Sash to the foot of the icefall. The next section varies in height between 45m and 60m. Climb the ice, keeping close to the right wall. Belays are possible, but it may be climbed as one pitch with a long rope. Above, the angle eases and the line of least resistance is followed to the plateau. *Diagram page 179.*

241 **Diadem** 210m IV

J. Brown and T. W. Patey   February 1964

A fine, hard climb, which follows the righthand of the prominent, twin icefalls.

Climb the snow gully of The Sash to the foot of the righthand icefall. Climb the icefall and the easy ground above to the foot of a long ice corner, which leads to easy-angled snow and the top. *Diagram page 179.*

242 **Fairy Godmother** 210m III

M. G. Geddes and N. C. Rayner   December 1970

Right of The Sash is a broken buttress with a prominent central snowfield. Near the right edge of this buttress is a steep, narrow chimney. Start midway between The Sash and this chimney, at a rightward-sloping ramp. Climb one pitch up the ramp, then up left by ramps and walls to the central snowfield. Climb a short gully with an ice pitch on the left, then a ramp going up left to an airy perch overlooking Diadem. Finish by the steep tower above. *Diagram page 179.*

23 The Inner Coire of Creag Meaghaidh

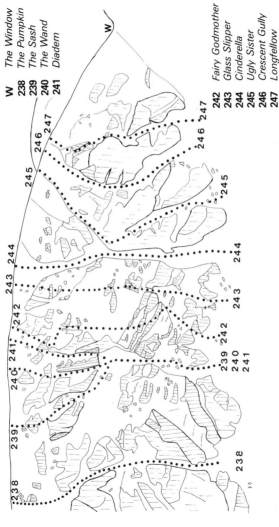

W	The Window
238	The Pumpkin
239	The Sash
240	The Wand
241	Diadem

242	Fairy Godmother
243	Glass Slipper
244	Cinderella
245	Ugly Sister
246	Crescent Gully
247	Longfellow

243   Glass Slipper   200m   III
I. A. MacEacheran and J. Knight   March 1964

The right side of the broken buttress with the central snowfield has the line of a steep, narrow chimney, just left of the prominent snow gully of Cinderella. Climb the chimney in two pitches to the central snowfield. Above, climb the central one of three breaks, with one ice pitch, to the top. *Diagram page 179.*

244   Cinderella   200m   I/II
T. W. Patey and W. Tout   February 1963

This is the prominent, straight snow gully in the centre of the Coire. It gives a pleasant climb on snow, with one or two short ice pitches early in the season. *Diagram page 179.*

The ramp leaving Cinderella at mid-height, on the right wall, gives the start of The Prow, III.

245   Ugly Sister   200m   III
M. G. Geddes and N. C. Rayner   December 1970

Well right of Cinderella, is the curving line of Crescent Gully. Between the two, is a snow ramp, slanting up left. Climb the ramp to a saddle, continue by the crest for 6m and traverse right to a better line leading up left to a crest. Climb the crest to the cornice, which may be difficult. *Diagram page 179.*

246   Crescent Gully   200m   II
J. Clarkson and R. J. Tanton   February 1968

This is the curving gully, mid-way between Cinderella and the Window. Climb up left on snow to an ice pitch, which leads to a snow bowl and the cornice. *Diagram page 179.*

247   Longfellow   200m   II
R. McMillan and G. S. Peet   March 1968

Right of Crescent Gully is another narrow gully. Climb this for 60m, move right, then left, over a short wall, to gain a groove system on the left, which leads to the crest of the buttress and so to the plateau. *Diagram page 179.*

248   **The Girdle Traverse**   c. 2,400m   III/IV

T. W. Patey   March 1969

Although a selective guide has little room for girdles, this unique route, immortalised as the "Crab Crawl" by the late Tom Patey, cannot be ignored. It crosses in four stages, initially climbed separately, the cliffs of Coire Ardair. For much of the way, it follows a natural line.

The traverse is done from left to right. Cross Bellevue Buttress by the ledge line of The Scene (II), and Pinnacle Buttress by Appolyon Ledge (II), spectacularly exposed. The third section, Post Horn Gallop (III), starts up the first pitch of The Last Post and follows a less obvious line rightwards, to finish near the top of Staghorn Gully. The final section, The Last Lap (III/IV), crosses the face of the Inner Coire, by descending below The Wand, via the upper part of The Sash and following an up and down traverse to the Window. Not shown on diagram.

26 The Post Face of Creag Meaghaidh

Photo: C. Stead

CREAG DUBH OF NEWTONMORE

Creag Dubh of Newtonmore, G.R. 670 958, is located on the north side of the A86 Spean Bridge to Newtonmore road, some 5km south-west of Newtonmore. The most useful map to the area is the O.S. Second Series sheet 35.

ACCESS

The crags are 5 to 10 minutes walk from the road. There are no access problems. Parking for cars is available in lay-bys below the cliffs.

ACCOMMODATION

There are two small campsites below the cliffs, on the north side of the road, the best being on a grassy knoll by the burn, some 75m left of the lay-by below the Central Wall. For those with transport, the fleshpots of Aviemore are not too distant, but Newtonmore itself supplies the usual amenities.

MOUNTAIN RESCUE

For rescue services, contact the Police. Dial 999. There is no public phone box near the cliffs, but there are several private houses.

THE CLIMBING

Although a roadside crag, Creag Dubh is a major rock climbing area in its own right, containing over 70 recorded routes up to 120m in length and mostly of a high order of difficulty. Indeed there are only a few routes below Very Severe in standard which are worth doing. Approximately half of the recorded routes are included in this guide. For information on other routes, consult the pages of the S.M.C. Journal and the guide to the "Eastern Outcrops and Creag Dubh", published by Highrange.

The surrounds of Creag Dubh are more pastoral than any other area included in this book and for the naturalist, the old woodlands around Creag Dubh offer a flora and fauna of great interest, including those natural climbers, the feral goats. One of the less savoury attraction is is the high number of rotting sheep carcasses.

The rock is a schist, fairly sound overall, but loose blocks are common. The climbs are clean, but some, especially those on Waterfall Wall, finish on steep, mixed rock and vegetation and it is often pleasanter to descend by abseil from a convenient tree. The climbing is on steep walls, with many roofs and overhangs and is strenuous in nature. The crags have a southerly aspect and a relatively dry climate, so that climbing is theoretically possible throughout the year and when higher crags are out of condition. The rock dries quickly after rain, but is very greasy when wet. One winter climb has been recorded.

Pegs are sometimes needed for main belays, but rarely now for aid. Any peg runners are usually in position.

Facing the road, the lowest crags are those of the Central Wall, with its highest section being the Great Wall. Left of this is a prominent waterfall, Oui Oui, which marks the left end of Waterfall Wall. Above and right of the Central Wall is Sprawl Wall with its many overhangs. Away to the left of the Central and Waterfall Walls, the rounded profile of Bedtime Buttress with its huge roof, pokes through the trees.

HISTORY

The first recorded climbs on Creag Dubh were done by H. Raeburn and C. Walker in November 1903. Writing in the S.M.C. Journal, Raeburn said "We did two climbs here. The first is up into a large over-hung chimney or cavern in the face, near its centre. The chimney comes to an end under the overhang, but we found our way out on the left to a mountain ash tree clinging to the face and thence straight up. Descending again we attacked a smaller, but sporting chimney, a little way to the east of the big one. This stopped in the same way as the first, but again we got out to the left. C. Walker who led then took us up the face above by steep and rotten grass ledges, which, but for the ice axe, we could not have ventured on." Presumably this refers to the gully just left of the Great Wall and possibly the line of Fred.

After this, the crag sank into oblivion, until in 1959, T. Sullivan and A. Parkin climbed Nutcracker Chimneys. Sullivan returned later in the same year with N. Collingham and climbed The Brute, a fine line which has become popular. Three years later, M. Owen and D. Gregory climbed Slanting Groove, a route which remained in obscurity because of its poor initial pitches. Dougal Haston appeared on the scene in 1964 when, with T. Gooding he climbed the impressive line of Inbred, a hard route up the steep part of the Great Wall, which became the local test piece. The next year, Haston and the Edinburgh Squirrels laid siege to the crag and in an explosion of activity they climbed over 30 routes.

Having developed so rapidly, there was a pause in exploration, but in 1967, The Hill was climbed by K. Spence and J. Porteous, a formidable climb of awe-inspiring steepness up the blank wall to the left of Inbred. Through into the seventies, a trickle of routes continued, but the wind of change sweeping Scottish climbing brought with it D. Cuthbertson who added several very fine and hard routes, including some of the most serious climbing on the crag. As well as new climbs, Cuthbertson and his friends eliminated much of the aid from the existing routes, so that Creag Dubh has reached a state of intensively developed respectability, offering routes of the highest standards of free climbing, comparable with the best anywhere.

BEDTIME BUTTRESS

Bedtime Buttress is the furthest left of the crags on Creag Dubh. It is divided into two sections by a vegetated groove. The climbs are described from right to left, beginning with the righthand section.

BEDTIME BUTTRESS—RIGHTHAND SECTION

The lower part of the buttress is steep and is separated from the slabby upper part by a terrace. The upper slabs are capped at their left end by the huge roof which is such a prominent feature.

249 **Gham** 76m Very Severe
D. Haston and Miss J. Heron May 1965

After a difficult "boulder problem" start, the climbing eases somewhat.

Start just right of the half-fallen birch tree which grows against the crag, below a jutting shelf. Gain the shelf with difficulty and traverse right to a deep corner which is climbed to a roof. Cross this on the left and climb a steep wall to a tree belay (20m). Either climb the wall on the left to a ledge below another wall, or climb the grass to the same point. Take the wall by a steep crack to a tree belay (23m). Finish by the slab to the right of the huge roof (33m). *Diagram page 186.*

250 **Porn** 71m Hard Very Severe
J. Porteous and M. Watson April 1970

From the half-fallen birch tree at the crag base, move 2m left. Either climb a wall for 3m and traverse right to a crack below a bulge, or gain the bulge directly from below. Climb the bulge and continue by a leftward trend until moves back right lead to a small cave (26m). Step right and climb a steep wall to a tree belay (12m). Finish by the slabs of Gham (33m). *Diagram page 186.*

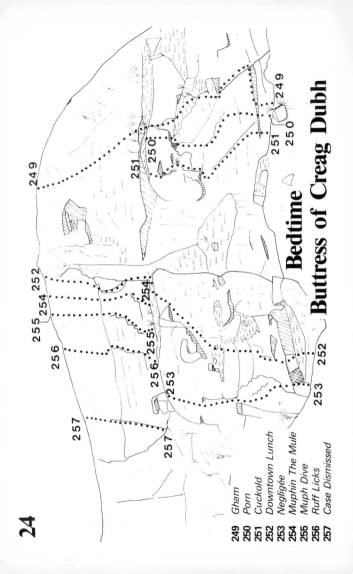

Bedtime Buttress of Creag Dubh

249 Gham
250 Porn
251 Cuckold
252 Downtown Lunch
253 Negligée
254 Muphin The Mule
255 Muph Dive
256 Ruff Licks
257 Case Dismissed

251 **Cuckold**   78m   Extremely Severe E1
D. Haston and J. Moriarty   May 1965

A good climb, originally using some aid, now free.

Start 5m left of the half-fallen birch tree, at a block against the wall. Above, is a thin crack running diagonally left. Gain the crack and follow it until a left traverse leads to a corner. Climb the corner to a tree and move left to a poor stance and belay (30m). Climb a quartz band to the roof, which is turned on the left and continue to a grass ledge (15m). Finish by the slabs of Gham (33m). *Diagram page 186.*

BEDTIME BUTTRESS—LEFTHAND SECTION

The lower part of this is shrouded in trees. It too, is divided by a terrace, above which is a short, steep wall, on which several very hard one-pitch climbs have recently been done. The climbs are described from right to left, beginning with the bottom tier.

252 **Downtown Lunch**   100m   Hard Very Severe
F. Harper, A. Ewing and A. McKeith   May 1965

Good climbing, spoilt by a scrappy middle section.

There is a cave, just left of the lowest rocks. Start just right of this, below the right end of some roofs. Climb to the roofs, traverse left and over a bulge and climb a wall to a belay (25m). Climb up and right to the terrace, passing below the big roof (45m). From the right end of the terrace, climb a bulge and an overhanging corner, to step left and finish by a slab (30m). *Diagram page 186.*

253 **Negligée**   39m   Severe
I. A. MacEacheran and R. S. Burnett   May 1965

Hard for its grade.

Start at the left end of the crag, just left of the cave. Climb into an overhung groove which leads onto a steep wall. Below a tree, traverse left round an edge and climb a corner to the terrace. *Diagram page 186.*

The following climbs start from the upper terrace.

254 **Muphin the Mule**   26m   Extremely Severe E1
D. Cuthbertson and D. Mullin   October 1977

Start at the right end of the terrace, at an overhanging corner, just left of the edge. Climb the corner and crack to a ledge and finish by a wall and slab above. *Diagram page 186.*

255 **Muph Dive**   30m   Extremely Severe E2
D. Bathgate and R. K. Holt   May 1965

A good climb, formerly aided in part and now free.

It climbs the prominent, stepped, overhanging corner near the right end of the terrace. Climb the corner and the wall above directly. *Diagram page 186.*

256 **Ruff Licks**   26m   Extremely Severe E3
D. Cuthbertson and R. Anderson   September 1977

This very strenuous route starts 10m left of Muph Dive, at the foot of a quartz crack. Go up and right to the crack which is climbed to a small tree. Go left and climb a crack to finish. *Diagram page 186.*

257 **Case Dismissed**   25m   Extremely Severe E3
D. Cuthbertson   October 1978

This strenuous route climbs the cracked, overhanging wall, well left of Ruff Licks and just left of a large flake. Climb up and right to a crack which is followed directly. *Diagram page 186.*

WATERFALL WALL

Waterfall Wall is defined on the left by the prominent waterfall of Oui Oui and on the right by the deep corner of Romp. To the left of the waterfall, some short routes have been recorded. Right of the waterfall, a terrace at 36m marks the end of the good climbing. From this terrace, descent by abseil from one of the trees is recommended. In the centre of the wall below the terrace is a prominent, overhung recess. Further right, 15m up the wall is a long tree-lined ledge. The routes are described from left to right.

258 **Oui Oui**   90m   Difficult
R. S. Burnett and A. McKeith   October 1965

Start in the corner right of the waterfall and climb this, moving left behind its upper part and finishing up left. Wet. *Diagram page 191.*

27 Oui Oui (Colin Grant). *Photo: C. Stead*

WINTER   III

M. Galbraith and R. Woodcock   1966

Under appropriate conditions of hard frost, this gives a very good climb up a great pillar of ice. The only recorded winter climb at Creag Dubh.

259   **Epar**   50m   Severe

D. Haston   May 1965

Start 15m right of the burn coming from the waterfall, at a shallow left-facing corner, below a prominent crack. Climb the corner to a grass ledge, pull into the crack and follow it to a big ledge and belay on the right (27m). Traverse right for 15m and climb a short corner to easy ground. *Diagram page 191.*

260   **Hayripi**   36m   Severe

D. Haston and M. Galbraith   June 1965

Left of the big overhung recess is a large roof at the top of the wall. Begin directly below this at a rightward-facing corner. Climb this to a good tree, step right and climb a groove which becomes a left-trending ramp, to finish just left of the big roof. Continue by the corner of Epar directly above, or abseil. *Diagram page 191.*

261   **Tip Off**   39m   Very Severe

D. Bathgate and I. A. MacEacheran   March 1965

A fine little climb, easy for its grade. It follows the groove in the left wall of the big overhung recess.

Start just right of a short, wide corner crack and climb a wall to a ledge. Cross the small overhang above and follow the groove. Below the big roof, gain a ledge on the left and finish by a thin crack in the overhangs directly above. *Diagram page 191.*

262   **Show Off**   51m   Hard Very Severe

D. Bathgate and J. Renny   October 1965

This climbs the overhanging wall above the left end of the long tree-lined ledge.

Climb a wall to a belay at the left end of the tree-lined ledge (15m). Step out left on to the wall and climb up left (peg runner) to a short slab which leads to a roof. Step right to a block and finish by the groove on the right. *Diagram page 191.*

25

Waterfall Wall of Creag Dubh

258	Oui Oui	263	Take Off
259	Epar	264	Smirnoff
260	Hayripi	265	Romp
261	Tip Off	266	Breakaway
262	Show Off		

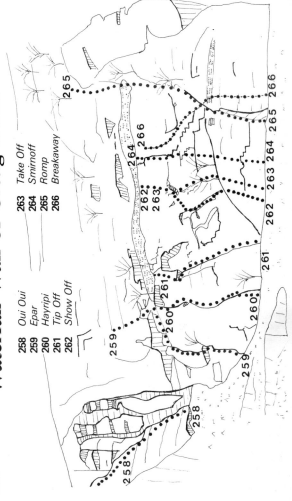

28 Smirnoff (Stuart Smith). *Photo: C. Stead*

263   **Take Off**   45m   Very Severe
D. Bathgate and J. Renny   October 1965

A pleasant route and easy for its grade, but on dubious rock.
Start below the tree-lined ledge at a point 5m right of its left end.
Climb the wall to a tree belay (15m). Follow a line of ledges which lead left and up to the skyline and climb this to easier ground and a tree belay on the terrace (30m). *Diagram page 191.*

264   **Smirnoff**   42m   Hard Very Severe
D. Bathgate and J. Brumfitt   November 1965

This is an excellent climb with some unusual moves. It follows the stepped, overhanging corner above the right end of the tree-lined ledge.
Start below the corner, 5m right of Take Off.
Climb the wall crossing a quartz overhang to the tree ledge (15m). Bridge up between a tree and the rock, cross the overhang and climb the corner (27m). *Diagram page 191.*

265   **Romp**   75m   Very Difficult
D. Haston   May 1965

Start at the prominent left-facing corner at the right end of Waterfall Wall. After a good first pitch the climbing deteriorates.
Climb the corner for 30m to a ledge. Continue by short walls and more broken ground to easy going. *Diagram page 191.*

266   **Breakaway**   60m   Hard Very Severe
D. W. Cuthbertson and F. Allison   September 1977

Start at the lefthand of two grooves in the wall right of Romp.
Climb the groove past a big block to belay on Romp (30m). Go up and climb a quartz crack on the left to a roof, turned on the left. Finish by a slab (30m). *Diagram page 191.*

THE CENTRAL WALL

Walking right from Waterfall Wall, two huge ribs, separated by gullies are passed. Both ribs have been climbed at Very Severe, but neither gives a good route. Stretching away right from here are the crags of the Central Wall, divided into the Great Wall (the lefthand and higher section) and the Lower Central Wall, which is the righthand and lower section.

The Great Wall is impressively steep. Its left end is defined by a deep gully, right of which is the prominent narrow arete of King Bee, to the immediate right of which is the vegetated chimney line of Nutcracker Chimneys, Very Severe. Towards the right end of the Great Wall, is a steep, smooth wall with the triangular niche of Inbred at 20m. The Great Wall is divided from the Lower Central Wall by the prominent, rightward-sloping rib line of Rib Direct.

The climbs are described from left to right, beginning with the Great Wall.

THE GREAT WALL

267   Men Only   66m   Extremely Severe E2
D. Cuthbertson and A. Taylor   September 1976

This fine route climbs a groove line on the right wall of the gully bounding the Great Wall on its left.

Scramble up the gully wall to a ledge and tree belay to the left of a green wall. Move right to a groove in the green wall and climb it, crossing an overhang to a ledge with a small tree. Move right and climb a crack and roof, to traverse left to a flake belay (36m). Climb the flake and wall to a roof, turned on the right to join King Bee. Step left and climb a corner and roof to easier ground (30m). *Diagram page 197.*

Between Men Only and the arete of King Bee is a big roof. This is crossed by the line of the very hard and serious Run Free, Extremely Severe E4.

268   King Bee   113m   Very Severe
D. Haston, J. Moriarty and A. Ewing   April 1965

This is the classic of the crag, giving fine climbing and situations.

Start at the left end of the Great Wall at a narrow arete, just left of the tree-choked chimney of Nutcracker Chimneys. Climb the arete, turning the overhang on the left to gain a tree and move right across the lip of the overhang to a ledge and belay (23m). Traverse left on to a steep wall and climb this to a tree belay (18m). Move left to a small bulge and climb this and the wall above to a cluster of roofs, which are climbed up, then right to a ledge with a big tree (36m). Ascend the bulge

29 King Bee Direct (Stuart Smith). *Photo: C. Stead*

behind the tree and climb the easier walls to the top (36m). *Diagram page 197.*

A harder direct start may be made by climbing the overhang on the first pitch, Hard Very Severe.

269   **Erse**   120m   Hard Very Severe

D. Haston, Miss J. Heron and J. Moriarty   May 1965

This climbs the wall right of the vegetated Nutcracker Chimneys. Originally aided, it now goes free.

Start just right of the chimney. Climb a groove and overhang and move right to a ledge. Move left and climb the wall to the roof (peg runner). Cross the roof and go left to a belay (30m). Climb the wall and a crack to belay below a roof (36m). Turn the roof on the left and climb a corner to a tree belay (25m). Easier climbing to the top. *Diagram page 197.*

270   **The Brute**   113m   Very Severe

T. Sullivan and N. Collingham   October 1959

Start at the same point as Erse. Climb the corner-groove, moving right to a belay at 12m. Traverse right and up below the overhangs to an overhanging crack, which is climbed to an earth ledge at 20m. Continue by the prominent corner above to a good ledge on the right (18m). Climb directly to a tree belay at 30m and finish by two slabs on the left (33m). *Diagram page 197.*

271   **Organ Grinder**   120m   Extremely Severe E1

K. V. Crocket and C. Stead   June 1971

This route takes a left-trending line, starting below the overhangs of the Brute and finishing between Erse and Nutcracker Chimneys.

Start well right of the trees to the right of the Brute and 10m left of some rusty rocks, at the foot of a blind crack. Climb 3m to a flake and follow a left-sloping crack for a few metres, until the wall can be climbed to a ledge and belay (20m). Move up, then right and climb a thin crack through the overhangs (as for the Brute). Go up a slab on the left to a ledge and belay (30m). Climb the wall above to the roof and traverse left to an overhanging recess (junction with Erse). Climb the overhang and then go up left to follow the right-bounding rib of Nutcracker Chimneys to a tree belay (40m). Find a way more easily through the overhangs above to the top (30m). *Diagram page 197.*

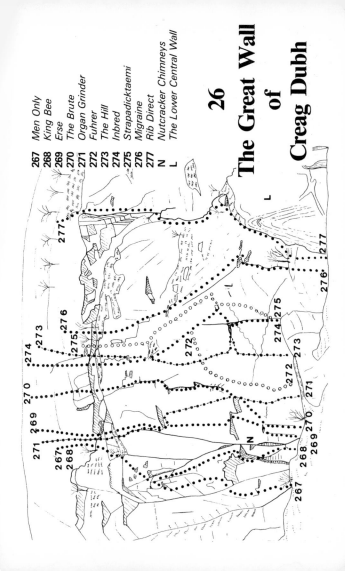

267 Men Only
268 King Bee
269 Erse
270 The Brute
271 Organ Grinder
272 Fuhrer
273 The Hill
274 Inbred
275 Strapadicktaemi
276 Migraine
277 Rib Direct
N   Nutcracker Chimneys
L   The Lower Central Wall

26

The Great Wall
of
Creag Dubh

272   **Fuhrer**   45m   Extremely Severe E4

D. W. Cuthbertson and I. Duckworth   June 1979

   Start just right of Organ Grinder.
   Climb to a rounded spike and up a quartz scoop going diagonally left to reach and stand on a block. Traverse right and up, over a bulge to a large spike, then climb up and left by a quartz blotch, stepping right to girdle ledge which leads right to a junction with Inbred. Finish by that route (see below). *Diagram page 197.*

273   **The Hill**   63m   Extremely Severe E2

K. Spence and J. Porteous   September 1967

   Right of Organ Grinder, the Great Wall is at its most impressive. The steep, rusty rocks give the line of The Hill, a fine and serious route.
   Climb the wall to a small ledge below a poor peg runner. Climb a groove above until a right traverse leads to the niche of Inbred, belay (18m). Traverse back left to line of weakness, trend up left to a small niche. Climb the wall above to a ledge and move right to belay on Inbred (30m). Climb a bulge and continue to a ledge and tree belay (15m). A further 45m of easy climbing leads to the top. *Diagram page 197.*

274   **Inbred**   100m   Hard Very Severe

D. Haston and T. Gooding   October 1964

   A fine steep route.
   Start at a projecting flake on a raised ledge towards the right end of the Great Wall, directly below the triangular niche. Climb the flake and the thin crack to a peg runner below the niche. Move up and left to the niche, then go up right to a ledge with a big loose block and bolt belay (21m). From the left end of the ledge, climb a bulge and follow a fault running diagonally left to a tree belay (33m). Move left and climb a wall to the top (45m). *Diagram page 197.*
   A direct finish, more in keeping with the standard of the first pitch may be made by climbing the crack rising from the roof of the niche and finishing by the last part of Strapadicktaemi (see below).

275   **Strapadicktaemi**   104m   Hard Very Severe

R. Anderson and D. Cuthbertson   September 1976

   A devious, but interesting route.
   Start as for Inbred, but after a metre or so, break out right by a thin

crack to a ledge and climb a groove and bulge, moving left to belay at the big block of Inbred (23m). Traverse right to a left-slanting crack, which follow to a left traverse and block below another crack (Inbred direct finish joins here). Climb the crack to easier ground (36m). Continue by any line to finish (45m). *Diagram page 197.*

276 **Migraine** 120m Hard Very Severe

I. A. MacEacheran and A. McKeith May 1965

Start near the far right end of the Great Wall, at a wall below a crack line leading to slabs, between Inbred and Rib Direct. Climb the wall to a ledge and follow an overhanging flake up right to gain the crack which leads to a comfortable ledge (21m). Climb a strenuous bulge above (crux) to the slabs and follow the left edge of these to a stance (36m). Climb to a terrace and take the easier upper walls to the top (63m), belays as required. *Diagram page 197.*

THE LOWER CENTRAL WALL

This wall, a lower continuation of the Great Wall, extends from Rib Direct, first as a steep wall, then a very prominent chimney, Cunnulinctus. A further steep wall and a huge ivy tree lead to its right extremity at a narrow gully known as Fred, Very Difficult. The walls on the right flank of the gully stretch a long way right, but are not worth climbing.

The climbs on the Lower Central Wall are short and, unless continuing to Sprawl Wall, descent may conveniently be made by abseil from a suitable tree, e.g. the one which overlooks the first pitch of Fred.

The climbs are described from left to right.

277 **Rib Direct** 90m Very Difficult

B. Halpin, T. Abbey and S. Tondeur Date unknown

This is the best route of its standard at Creag Dubh, giving good climbing, apart from its second pitch.

To the right of the highest part of the Great Wall, a prominent rib runs up rightwards. Start below the rib at a black wall and climb this on good holds to a ledge with a big tree. Take the rib on the right to a tree belay (30m). Traverse left 3m, climb a short crack and broken ground to a tree (24m). Gain and climb the rib on the right (36m). *Diagram page 197 and 200.*

N

The Lower Central Wall of Creag Dubh

27

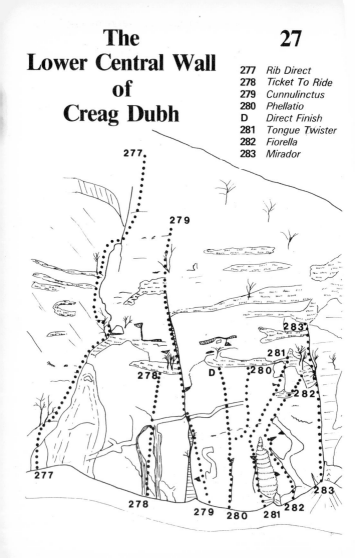

278 **Ticket to Ride**   36m   Extremely Severe E2

D. W. Cuthbertson and A. Taylor   September 1976

A fine steep pitch, poorly protected.

A huge quartz vein runs leftward up the very steep wall at the left end of the Lower Wall. Start just left of the vein at a black streak which gives the line of the route. Climb up and right across the quartz to a flake and gain a small niche. Step left and climb the wall to a big ledge and tree belay. *Diagram page 200.*

279 **Cunnulinctus**   72m   Very Severe

R. S. Burnett and A. McKeith   October 1965

Easy for the grade, this route more or less climbs the prominent chimney in the centre of the wall.

Start at the right wall of the chimney. Climb diagonally left to join the chimney at the holly tree. Continue by the chimney, or the wall on its right to a tree belay (36m). Climb a chimney above (36m). *Diagram page 200.*

280 **Phellatio**   36m   Very Severe

A. Ewing and I. A. MacEacheran   May 1965

Combined with the Direct Finish, this is a sustained and strenuous route.

Start just right of the chimney of Cunnulinctus at a broken groove. Climb the groove, trending left to a ledge at 15m, belay. Traverse right and climb a crack to easy ground. *Diagram page 200.*

DIRECT FINISH   Very Severe

K. V. Crocket and C. Stead   June 1972

Better and harder than the original.

From the belay at 15m, continue directly 10m, then slightly left to easy ground. *Diagram page 200.*

281 **Tongue Twister**   30m   Very Severe

D. M. Jenkins and C. Stead   July 1970

Hard for its grade, this starts at the groove, just left of the holly tree. Climb the groove and cross the overhang, to trend left to a block and back right to a ledge with a small bush. Continue to a higher ledge and tree belay. *Diagram page 200.*

282 **Fiorella** 26m Very Severe
F. Harper, A. McKeith and J. Knight   November 1965

An excellent pitch, easy for its grade.

Start at a groove right of the ivy tree. Climb the groove, cross a small overhang and move left, then right to a tree belay. *Diagram page 200.*

283 **Mirador** 36m Severe
I. A. MacEacheran, J. Knight and R. S. Burnett   May 1965

This route climbs the left-bounding arete of the gully of Fred in two pitches. *Diagram page 200.*

SPRAWL WALL

Sprawl Wall, well named, is the line of crags above and right of the Central Wall. From right to left, its main features are firstly, a belt of slabs, separated on its left from a black-streaked, overhanging wall, by a deep corner. Left of this is the very prominent left-sloping diagonal fault of Slanting Groove, Hard Very Severe. Left of this groove, comes an area of greyish rock, with a small projecting buttress at its left end. Well left of this, an area of white-marked rock with a huge roof above gives the line of Gang Bang and the end of the climbing on Sprawl Wall.

The climbs are described from right to left.

284 **Tree Hee** 65m Severe
H. Small and J. Graham   April 1965

This route, unusually for Creag Dubh, gives enjoyable slab climbing.

Start at the right end of Sprawl Wall, at the foot of the slabs, just left of a grassy groove. Make a left, rising traverse above an overhanging wall, towards the left edge, until a shallow corner can be climbed to a ledge with a holly tree on the right edge of the deep corner (30m). Move up right past the holly tree and go straight up the slab to an overlap, traverse left to a ledge and finish up a wall (35m). *Diagram page 204.*

A variation may be made to the second pitch, by following the left edge of the slabs, after passing the holly tree.

Photo: C. Stead

30 Jump So High, pitch two (Ed Jackson).

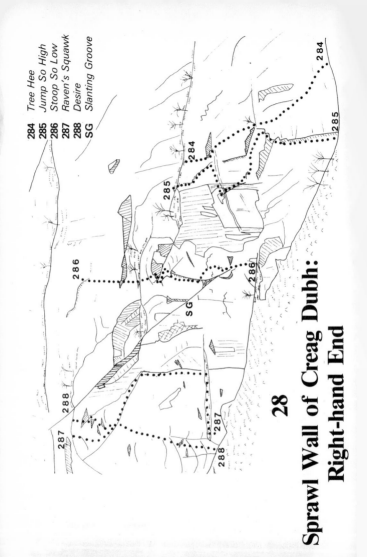

284	Tree Hee
285	Jump So High
286	Stoop So Low
287	Raven's Squawk
288	Desire
SG	Slanting Groove

28

**Sprawl Wall of Creag Dubh:
Right-hand End**

285 **Jump So High**   81m   Extremely Severe E1

F. Harper, A. McKeith and A. Ewing   May 1965

A fine climb, formerly using aid, now free. It climbs the overhanging wall, left of the slabs.

Start at the deep corner separating the slabs from the wall. Climb the corner to the tree belay on Tree Hee (30m). Follow the slabby ramp up left to a belay at the foot of an overhanging wall (21m). Climb the wall to a ledge and belay (12m). Go right and climb the edge of the slabs to finish (18m). *Diagram page 204.*

VARIATION   Hard Very Severe

K. Spence and J. Porteous   Summer 1969

An easier variation to pitch three. Instead of climbing the overhanging wall, traverse right and climb a crack to the belay below the last pitch of the original.

286 **Stoop So Low**   66m   Hard Very Severe

K. Spence and J. Porteous   September 1967

A good climb.

Start left of Jump So High, at a huge pink flake on a little rib, just left of a smooth grey wall and right of the foot of Slanting Groove. Climb a small groove to the left and follow a line of walls and ledges to a shallow scoop below a broken corner. Go left and climb the corner to a ledge (36m). Climb a small slab on the left, traverse right and climb the overhang at a break, to reach a ledge (12m). Finish by the wall above (18m). *Diagram page 204.*

287 **Raven's Squawk**   120m   Severe

M. Harcus and G. Anderson   June 1965

A good route, hard for its grade.

It climbs a left-slanting diagonal ramp, approximately parallel to and left of the final, prominent groove of Slanting Groove. Start at greyish rocks, right of a small projecting buttress.

There is a long grass ledge a few metres off the ground. Gain the right end of this and climb up and right, to follow a wall and groove to a ledge (30m). Move left and climb the ramp to a ledge (45m). Continue by the ramp until it fades and take the wall and easier ground to the top (45m). *Diagram page 204.*

288 **Desire**   72m   Extremely Severe E2

D. W. Cuthbertson and I. Duckworth   June 1979

This route follows a line of grooves to the left of Raven's Squawk, climbing the overhangs directly. It coincides for one pitch with an earlier and aided route. Start at the righthand side of the small, projecting buttress.

Climb up the right side of the small buttress to a ledge (24m). From the right end of the ledge, gain a groove with a slabby right wall. Climb this and continue up and right to a stance on Raven's Squawk (24m). Traverse left and up to an old peg beneath an overlap. Pull over this and up to ledge below roof. Turn the roof on the right, then back left along an overhung shelf to finish directly over the final overhang to a tree (24m). *Diagram page 204.*

289 **Gang Bang**   54m   Very Severe

F. Harper and A. McKeith   May 1965

An excellent climb.

Near the left end of Sprawl Wall is a white-marked face, with a huge roof at its top. A line of shelves runs up, from right to left and gives the line of the route.

From the lowest rocks of the face, move right to a grass ledge in a corner. Go up and left to a bulge and climb it (peg runner) to a higher shelf, which leads left to a ledge and belay (24m). Continue up left to a large overhang and climb it on big holds (peg runner). Follow shelves up left to a grass ledge and finish up a short wall to a tree belay (30m). Scramble to the top. Not shown on diagram.

The first pitch may be started more directly by gaining the bulge from below, harder.

INDEX OF ROUTES

GARBH BHEINN OF ARDGOUR

BEN NEVIS

POLLDUBH CRAGS

NOTES

NOTES

NOTES

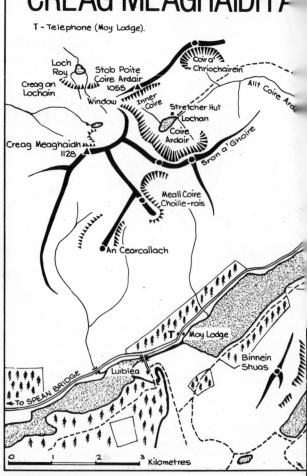

CREAG MEAGHAIDH A

T - Telephone (Moy Lodge).

Loch Roy
Creag an Lochain
Stob Poite Coire Ardair 1055
Window
Inner Coire
Coir a' Chriochairein
Allt Coire Arda
Stretcher Hut
Lochan
Coire Ardair
Creag Meaghaidh 1128
Sron a'Ghoire
Meall Coire Choille-rais
An Cearcallach
Moy Lodge
Binnein Shuas
Luiblea
← To SPEAN BRIDGE

0   1   2   3   Kilometres